Designers, Visionaries and Other Stories

Designers, Visionaries and Other Stories

A Collection of Sustainable Design Essays

Edited by Jonathan Chapman and Nick Gant

London • Sterling, VA

First published by Earthscan in the UK and USA in 2007

ISBN-13: 978-1-84407-413-6 Hardback
                978-1-84407-412-9 Paperback
Typeset by Safehouse Creative
Printed and bound in the UK by Cromwell Press, Trowbridge
Cover design by Jonathan Chapman

For a full list of publications please contact:

Earthscan
8–12 Camden High Street
London, NW1 0JH, UK
Tel: +44 (0)20 7387 8558
Fax: +44 (0)20 7387 8998
Email: earthinfo@earthscan.co.uk
Web: www.earthscan.co.uk

22883 Quicksilver Drive, Sterling, VA 20166-2012, USA

Earthscan publishes in association with the International Institute for Environment and Development

A catalogue record for this book is available from the British Library

        Library of Congress Cataloging-in-Publication Data

Designers, visionaries and other stories : an anthology of sustainable design essays / edited by
Jonathan Chapman and Nick Gant.
            p. cm.
        Includes bibliographical references and index.
        ISBN–13: 978-1-84407-413-6 (hardback : alk. paper)
        ISBN–10: 1-84407-413-7 (hardback : alk. paper)
        ISBN–13: 978-1-84407-412-9 (pbk. : alk. paper)
        ISBN–10: 1-84407-412-9 (pbk. : alk. paper)
    1. Sustainable design. I. Chapman, Jonathan, 1974– II. Gant, Nick. NK1520.D47 2007
    745.2–dc22

                                                        2007009558

This book is dedicated to Norman Gant

Contents

Chapter 3 Design Redux   56

Stuart Walker

Chapter 4 The Scenario of a Multi-local Society: Creative Communities, Active Networks and Enabling Solutions   76

Ezio Manzini

Chapter 5 Relative Abundance: Fuller's Discovery That the Glass Is Always Half Full   96

John Wood

List of Figures and Tables

Figures

Tables

List of Contributors

Jonathan Chapman and Nick Gant are co-directors of the Inheritable Futures Laboratory (IF:Lab) – a sustainable design research facility at the University of Brighton, UK. Jonathan is a senior lecturer in three dimensional design at the University of Brighton and author of *Emotionally Durable Design* (Earthscan, 2005). Nick is the subject leader of the three dimensional design programme at the University of Brighton and director of award-winning design practice BoBo Design. See www.brighton.ac.uk/arts/if_laboratory for more information.

Dr Kate Fletcher is a freelance eco design consultant and a leading specialist in sustainable fashion and textiles. Over the last decade, Kate's work has been a mix of research, consultancy, design practice and teaching with multinationals, non-governmental organizations (NGOs) and independent designers as well as in universities. Her most recent work has developed the idea of fast and slow clothes. For more information see www.katefletcher.com.

Alastair Fuad-Luke practises as a sustainable design facilitator, lecturer and writer. He is senior lecturer for the MA in Sustainable Product Design and the BA in Product Design Sustainable Futures at University College for the Creative Arts, Farnham, UK, and has lectured in the US, New Zealand and Australia. He is author of *The Eco-Design Handbook* (2002, 2005), an international best seller, and Vice-President of SlowLab, a not-for-profit organization encouraging 'slow design'. Currently he manages Design Education & Sustainability (DEEDS), a European Union funded project, and works as a facilitator/consultant for clients in Denmark, the US and the UK.

Ezio Manzini is professor of design at the Politecnico di Milano. He deals with strategic design and design for sustainability, with a focus on scenario building and solution development. Some results from his recent works appear in *Sustainable Everyday* (Manzini and Jégou (eds), 2003, Edizioni Ambiente), and in several papers (some of which can be found at www.sustainable-everyday.net/manzini/).

Stuart Walker was recently appointed professor and co-director of Imagination@Lancaster, Lancaster University, UK. Previously he was professor of industrial design at the postgraduate

Faculty of Environmental Design, University of Calgary, Canada, where he served successively as associate dean (academic) and associate dean (research), and as adjunct professor of engineering. He is also visiting professor of sustainable design at Kingston University, UK. His writings on sustainable design have been published internationally and his propositional designs have been exhibited in Canada, the UK and Italy. He serves on the editorial boards of several design journals, and is adviser to the UK's 'Design for the 21st Century' initiative. His book *Sustainable by Design: Explorations in Theory and Practice* was published by Earthscan, 2006.

John Wood is professor of design at Goldsmiths University of London. He has written over 100 papers and articles on ethics and design in the age of over-consumption. These include an edited book, *The Virtual Embodied* (1998, Routledge) and *The Design of Micro-Utopias; Thinking Beyond the Possible* (2007, Gower). He currently leads an Engineering and Physical Sciences Research Council (EPSRC)/Arts and Humanities Research Council (AHRC) funded project that explores 'Design Synergy as an Outcome of the Practice of Metadesign'. John is also co-editor of *The Journal of Writing in Creative Practice* (Intellect Books), and co-founder of the Attainable Utopias Network (see http://attainable-utopias.org/).

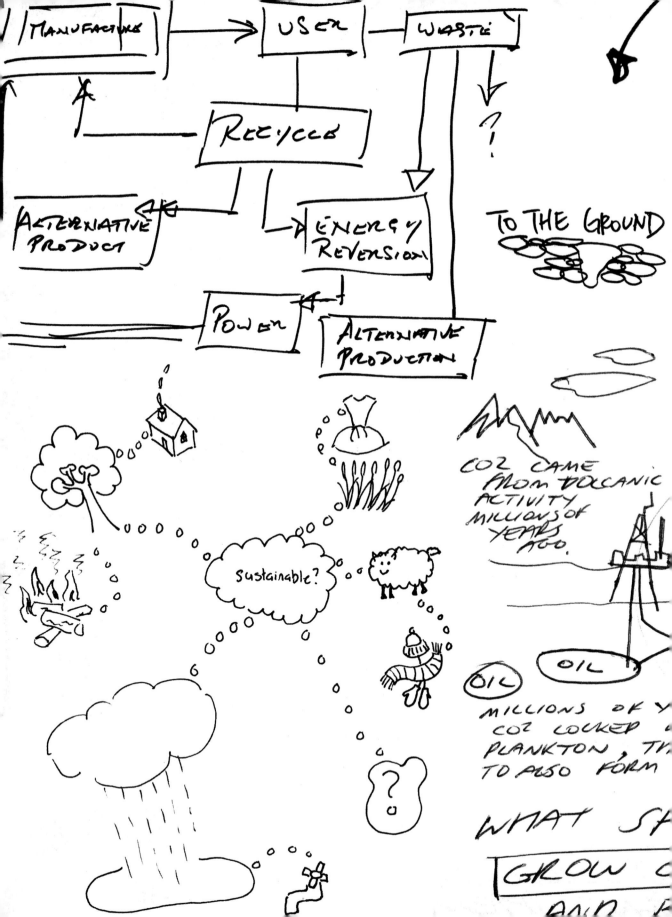

MANUFACTURE → USER → WASTE

RECYCLE

ALTERNATIVE PRODUCT

ENERGY REVERSION

POWER

ALTERNATIVE PRODUCTION

?

TO THE GROUND

CO2 CAME FROM VOLCANIC ACTIVITY MILLIONS OF YEARS AGO.

Sustainable?

OIL

OIL

MILLIONS OF Y
CO2 LOCKED
PLANKTON, TH
TO ALSO FORM

WHAT SH

GROW

AND

Foreword

Are designers guilty of killing the planet? Eighty per cent of the environmental impact of the products and buildings that surround us is determined at the design stage, after all. The ways we have designed the world force most people to waste stupendous quantities of matter and energy in their daily lives. Bruce Nussbaum, North America's most prominent design commentator, has flagged an emerging backlash against design. 'Designers suck!' he wrote in *Business Week*. 'Designers suck because they are IGNORANT, especially about sustainability. The rap against designers is that they design CRAP that hurts the planet' (www.businessweek.com/innovate/NussbaumOnDesign/archives/2007/03/are_designers_t.html).

There are three ways for designers to respond to the charge that they are personally responsible for trashing the biosphere: argue the toss; cringe with guilt; or become part of the solution. I favour the third way, which is why books like this one have such an important role to play.

Designers could argue that it's unfair to blame them for the climate change mess because they are just doing their job when they design a laptop computer that consumes a thousand times more resources in its manufacture than it weighs on your lap; or a mail-shot whose printing and distribution consumes vast amounts of matter and energy, and that its millions of recipients did not ask for; or when the design of a food display for a shop burns 15 times more energy than an office; or when a spectacularly designed dollar trade show stand ends up in a skip after three days. One could argue that, while regrettable, these wasteful and egregious projects were commissioned by a client – so why not give them a hard time, too?

A second response to the charge of biocide would be to retire to a monastery and repent. For designers, the monastery would ideally be located at Hua Hin in Thailand and be designed by John Pawson. This approach lacks credibility in two respects: the high per diem cost of such a strategy would be ruinous for all but a few celebrity designers; and besides, designers are notoriously bad at leaving things well alone and would quickly get bored with the contemplative life.

A third alternative to a lifelong guilt trip is for designers to wise up to the fact that there's a gigantic opportunity here. Someone has to redesign the structures, institutions and processes that drive the economy along. Someone has to transform the material, energy and resource flows that, unchecked, will finish us. That's a lot of work. This work is not really about green products, nor is it about influencing people's behaviour.

Most of the environmental impact of the products, services and infrastructures that surround us is determined at the design stage. Not at the point of purchase. And not at the point of use. It's hard to buy green, or be green, if the ways in which daily life is organized force you into *un*-green behaviour. Posters and ad campaigns that tell people to behave sustainably are a pointless diversion.

A second caveat: transformation underway is not a private project for the design industry or, worse, the 'creative class'. Transformation on the scale we are now embarked on won't happen if we approach it top-down or outside in. If you find yourself designing emergency shelters for poor black people from the comfort of a Soho design studio, you are not up to speed on an important change: sustainable design means the *co*-design of daily life with the people who are living it.

The most important reason to be out there, doing it on site, is that most elements of a sustainable world already exist. Some of those elements are technological solutions. Some are to be found in the natural world, thanks to millions of years of natural evolution. The majority are social practices – some of them very old ones – learned by other societies and in other times.

From this insight flows the idea of designers as global hunter-gatherers of models, processes and ways of living that already exist. Or used to. A big part of sustainable design is about sharing information about pre-existing solutions that have been proven to work. Creative design practice these days is about adapting solutions found in one context for use in another.

The problem is that the collective knowledge footprint of sustainable design is still tiny in a global context. And it is growing far too slowly relative to the time available for us to turn things around. This is why we have to crack the distribution question: how do we ensure that knowledge about sustainable practices is available where and when it is needed?

As scavenger-innovators, a first response to the question should be to ask another: who has cracked a similar distribution question in the past? How might we learn from, or piggyback on, *their* success? Three existing distribution channels strike me as being full of potential: grassroots activism, global business and religion.

The first is grassroots activism. According to Paul Hawken (www.worldchanging. com/archives/005670.html) over 1 million non-profit organizations and 100 million people daily work for the preservation and restoration of life on Earth. For Hawken, 'it's the single biggest movement on the planet'. It may be a big movement, but it lacks coherence. Yes, hundreds of millions of people now agree that something must be done to avert climate change, but when they – we – ask: 'where do I join?', the answer, with a million organizations to choose from, is by no means obvious.

The approach I advocate to designers is this: don't start a new organization. Find a well-organized one with good local roots and join that one. Offer them your scavenger-innovator design skills. Help them become expert at choosing between the multiple solutions on offer, or that can be found – including adjacent organizations.

A second distribution system that already exists is global business. Some multinationals are moving much faster on measures to avoid climate change than most governments – and all politicians. Patrick Cescau, for example, Group Chief Executive of Unilever (www.unilever.com/Images/ir_pc_montreux091006_tcm13-70144.pdf), has committed his company to the application of 'new design principles' that would 'progressively drive down our usage of resources and move towards ever more sustainable consumption'. Easy to say, of course; harder to do. I asked a couple of people in Unilever about this pledge. It sounds as if many of Cescau's 234,000 colleagues remain vague, to put it mildly, about what these 'new design principles' are – let alone how they are to be implemented.

But that just means there's an opportunity here. Unilever trades in most countries of the world. If they are in the market for sustainable design principles, it seems to me we should provide them.

A third distribution system for knowledge and sustainable design is religion. World religions have practised knowledge distribution for thousands of years. Not all of these churches' day to day behaviours were admirable, it's true. And some of their contemporary belief systems sit squarely in the enemy camp. Many devout people – by some estimates, 40 per cent of the world's population – believe fervently in apocalyptic 'end of days' scenarios and await climate-induced catastrophe with eager anticipation.

But not all. A growing number of evangelical Christians is engaging with aspects of 'environmental ministry' and some Christian organizations are downright militant participants in discussions of climate change policy. In the UK, Christian Aid has become a powerful advocate of science-based environmental policy and a critic of government dissembling (www.christian-aid.org.uk/ indepth/0702_climate/missingcarbon.pdf). Working with churches is not principally an ethical move. It's important to me that churches have widespread distribution networks and can also be great organizers.

NGOs, multinational businesses and churches may sound like unlikely bedfellows for designers – but these are unlikely times.

John Thackara
www.doorsofperception.com
www.dott07.com
www.thackara.com

Acknowledgements

We would like to thank John Thackara, Ezio Manzini, Alastair Fuad-Luke, Kate Fletcher, Stuart Walker and John Wood for their valuable contribution to this book. In addition, we would like to thank the 1000's of individuals who contributed a drawing, vision or diagram depicting their individual perception of sustainable design, many of which feature within this book.

We would also like to thank the following individuals and organizations for their contributions and support; Pete Massey, Alice Brown and Helen Horten-Smith of Reed Exhibitions (100% Design), Anne Boddington, Professor Bruce Brown, Dr Catherine Harper and Professor Jonathan Woodham of the University of Brighton's Faculty of Arts and Architecture; David White of the Knowledge Exchange; Ian Rudge; James McAdam, Seb Oddi and Oscar Wanless; Richard Morris of InQbate; Tamsine Green, Camille Adamson and Alison Kuznets of Earthscan.

Finally, we would like to thank Ming Ming & Jasper, and Tanya, Billy & Nell for their patience, understanding and support throughout the research, development and writing of this book.

List of Acronyms and Abbreviations

AHRC	Arts and Humanities Research Council
AFH	Architecture For Humanity
BBC	British Broadcasting Corporation
BP	British Petroleum
CSR	Corporate Social Responsibility
DEFRA	UK Department for Environment, Food and Rural Affairs
Devt	development
DJSI	Dow Jones Sustainability Indexes
DTI	Department of Trade and Industry
EAD	European Academy of Design
EMUDE	Emerging User Demands
EPSRC	Engineering and Physical Sciences Research Council
EU	European Union
FRN	Furniture Re-use Network
FTSE	Financial Times Stock Exchange
GDP	gross domestic product
HiCS	Highly Customized Solutions
ICT	information and communication technology
MDF	medium density fibreboard
MIT	Massachusetts Institute of Technology
MP3	Mpeg Layer 3
MPEG	Moving Picture Experts Group
NL	the Netherlands
PD	participatory design
PET	polyethylene terepthalate
SED	sustainable everyday project
SPD	sustainable product design
TBL	triple bottom line
TTL	triple top line
UCD	user-centred design
WBCSD	World Business Council for Sustainable Development
WEEE	Waste Electrical and Electronic Equipment

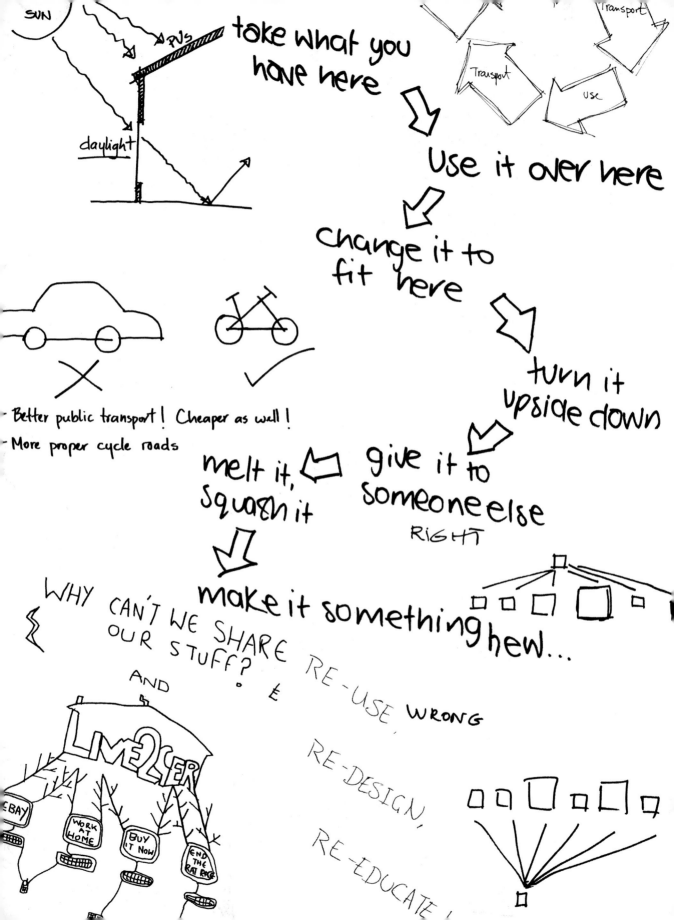

SUN

PVs

daylight

take what you have here

Transport

Transport

Use

Use it over here

change it to fit here

turn it upside down

✗

✓

- Better public transport! Cheaper as well!
- More proper cycle roads

melt it, squash it

give it to someone else

RIGHT

make it something new...

WHY CAN'T WE SHARE OUR STUFF?

AND

RE-USE, WRONG

RE-DESIGN,

RE-EDUCATE!

LIVE2ER

EBAY

WORK AT HOME

BUY IT NOW

END THE RAT RACE

Chapter 1

JONATHAN CHAPMAN & NICK GANT

Introduction

The sustainable design context

Although sustainable design could be considered a relatively young discipline, general concern for the environment is nothing new; it is possible to trace back observations that describe the impact of human endeavours on the natural world to the 13th century – German theologian Meister Eckhart was amongst the first to identify the emergence of our negative impact on the environment. Ancient animistic cultures considered themselves an integral part of natural systems and had a more direct and symbiotic relationship with Nature, which made their impacts (positive and negative) upon the immediate environment more tangible and visceral, and this undoubtedly affected the way they perceived both the environment, and their place within it. However, in more contemporary situations our species has moved to separate itself from natural systems, turning Nature into an *other* – the more that Nature is objectified as an external entity, then the more one is separated from it.

Today, perhaps as a direct consequence of our streamlined and automated lifestyles, we seem to place ourselves beyond *all this*. In the constructed environment, Nature is frequently perceived as an opposing force; a random unpredictable realm in constant rotational flux that must be beaten down and controlled. In contrast, seeing the interrelation between things, the cause and effect and the linkages that connect seemingly disparate elements are all part of a *sustainable perception*. This extends beyond the disconnected and closed attitudes often adopted by contemporary consumer cultures, to which design contributes. However, we are as dependent today on Nature as we have ever been and the illusion we have constructed around ourselves has deceived us into thinking we have conquered it, and become its masters. Yet, beneath the glossy surface of this *mirage of progress* ecological decay on an unprecedented scale has been steadily gestating.

So why has sustainability appeared so late on the radar? Perhaps it is because we can now see that the ecological changes happening around us are having an immediate and tangible impact on human health, prosperity and happiness. Furthermore, sustainability is becoming increasingly quantifiable in economic terms. Though this may be cynically perceived as *anthropocentrism at work*, the move away from the charitable, altruistic guise that is often portrayed by sustainable action may actually be more productive. In addition, climate change and an increase in energy and material cost can no longer be ignored – economically or environmentally.

Within the last 50 years numerous strategic approaches to sustainable design, production and consumption have been developed and deployed, with varying degrees of success. Conventionally, sustainable design is understood as a collection of strategies, which broadly include: products designed for ease of disassembly and recycling; designing with appropriate materials to ensure a reduction in environmental impact; design that optimizes energy consumption and considers options for alternate sources of power; and design that considers longer lasting products both in terms of their physical and emotional endurance, to name but a few. Although there are many strategic approaches to sustainable design that make key contributions to the discipline, it is certainly not all figured out, and essential debate continues to question and explore the most effective ways and means of working with it. This book aims to unpack some of these debates, to both question current approaches and facilitate the pioneering of new strategies.

One thing is for sure: the only universal constant is that of perpetual change. The ebb and flow of the tides, the erosion of the coastline or the continual fluctuation in global temperature – nothing stays the same, and it has always been this way. It is therefore essential that we too continue to evolve and change, as the environment evolves and changes in reaction to us. Indeed, without human presence, the Earth *will* heal itself, eventually. When described in this way, you could conclude that 'sustainable design is not rocket science'. After all, the planet doesn't actually need saving – just saving from us perhaps? So, we just need to find ways that enable us to continue as a species, but in a (more) sustainable way that places as little pressure on the biosphere as (humanly) possible.

Back in the early 20th century, in the heady innovation-days of Henry Ford, the favoured term 'design' meant creation, progression, development and the production of newer and better interpretations of everyday life. Today, we are back there, only now it is 'sustainable' design that signifies creation, progression and development, and presents the real opportunities for visionaries and heroes to emerge. It could even be said that, in today's new and enlightened age of sustainable awareness, design has become a lazy and somewhat cosmetic practice that erodes consumer consciousness to nurture promiscuous cultures of more, more and yet more. Yet whether the 'disease' or the 'cure', once again design has a central role to play in achieving a new and sustainable future. In terms of 'sustainability' therefore, design could be seen as the 'perpetrator' of whimsy, trend and transience. In this way, it may be asserted that 'sustainable' design *is* the cure – the antithesis of design's disease-like presence; the stocking-clad superhero that swoops in at the last minute to whisk us off that crumbling ledge.

Sustainable design is about criticism. Essentially, it is an edgy culture that reinvigorates design with the ethos of debate that was once the hallmark of creative practice. Situated well within the comfort zone of an ever-hungry consumer society, the daily throughput of products born of trend-driven design slip quietly through the net, unchallenged, while their 'sustainable' counterparts, by default, seem to invite criticism due to their participation in what is a *critical* process; the 'wagging finger' that baulks at any given product failing to achieving 100% sustainability often bullishly attacks any claim of environmental improvement. This mode of disruptive and non-inclusive assault is unnerving to many designers, and does not help to encourage designers to engage in more sustainable practice. Therefore, a less *bold* designer may remain perfectly content to 'piggyback' trends as a means to achieve immunity from such criticism. This could be described simply as 'lazy', as comforts await this breed of practitioner through the immediacy, low expectation and overall achievability of this prevailing mode of design. Sustainable design is not about this. Rather, it is a vibrant, dynamic and forward-looking discipline that questions why things are the way they are, and proposes how they could, and should be. Furthermore, for all its demands, sustainable design (beyond ecological benefits) offers creative sustenance, enduring meaning and genuine integrity to those who are willing to engage with it.

It may be proposed that the term *sustainable design* suggests that it is a 'thing', an 'other' that must be acquired and learnt in order for it to occur; an ethically enlightened destiny that must be aspired to by those practitioners and researchers who have reached 'that place' in their career. In fact, sustainable design can actually happen inadvertently, when it is not meant to. Is this still sustainable design? To put it another way, just because someone does not deliberately set out to achieve it, does not mean that it won't be achieved. Conversely, just because someone sets out to achieve it, does not necessarily mean that it will be achieved. Thus, the same dichotomy is constructed that is present in all areas of the sustainable debate; namely, is it sustainable or not, green or not, good or not, 100 per cent sustainable or not? Perhaps, therefore, the term 'sustainable design' is in itself unhelpful, as it tends to suggest that all other practice is unsustainable, and thus the aforementioned polarizations are further reinforced.

Sustainable design is generally considered a specialist approach to design *proper* – an extra (yet fully integrated) set of issues to be considered when planning, developing and producing objects, spaces and experiences. This *can* be non-inclusive (exclusive) and often serves to isolate and marginalize those that do, and those that do not. At this point, a false opposition is often created, where *sustainable design* and *design* split into two different camps, with 'apparently' different agendas. Despite this dualism, the work of the 'unsustainable' design camp is sometimes *inadvertently* more sustainable than that of the 'sustainable' design camp. The fundamentals of efficiency, for example, can often synchronize well with the motivations of sustainable design practice; reductions in material usage, driven primarily by cost, often afford a secondary (yet nonetheless impactful) improvement in sustainability. Speed, too, can be a catalyst to efficiency; the much criticized digital age, with its frictionless action may well take us closer to achieving sustainability than a lawnmower made from reclaimed steel could ever do. A false opposition perhaps, but essential notions of efficiency are often compatible with sustainable systems.

So why design anything at all?

There is a seemingly infinite range of means through which sustainability might be approached, as a designer today. Yet despite this diversity, the damning question poked in the face of most designers when approaching sustainability, is 'Why design anything at all?' At first, this might seem like an insightful and appropriate proposal, born as a natural consequence of sustainable design discourse, with its heart so firmly rooted in the reduction and minimization of impact. However, on closer inspection we see that consumption is both a natural and integral facet of human behaviour. Human behaviours are at the motivational core of today's production and consumption cycles and, as a sustainable designer, you ignore this at your peril. Furthermore, human behaviours should not be seen simply as the cause of all problems. Too often, consumer behaviours are fought against, and the natural train of thought that drives them is rebelled against and boycotted. In this context, one consequence of considering sustainability is often the conclusion *not* to consume, *not* to have – and to do without. Yet, this knee-jerk response to the problems we face flies in the face of our deep motivations as a species – to create, to produce and to consume. Problems arise when these deep motivations are expressed physically (e.g. objects, materials and new technologies), as opposed to metaphysically (e.g. stories, ideas and friendships).

In this respect, asking people to stop consuming is a pointless endeavour, when what we should be pursuing is redirective behaviour, which steers consumers towards greener, and more sustainable, alternatives (just as the response to the AIDS pandemic is not to try and stop the world having sex, but rather, to think about safer ways for individuals to go about it). This may well be a more favourable consumer destiny than asking people to do without, which is rather like asking a vampire to stop sucking blood. As with Dracula, our desire to consume is not necessarily *our fault*, and the sooner we come to terms with this, the sooner we can move forward; doom and gloom cultures of guilt and self-loathing are deeply counterproductive in terms of real progress. Sustainable design methodologies that fail to accommodate human desire are useless unless consumers actually embrace them, engage with them and essentially invest in them.

Is it possible for designers to change human behaviour? The designer's job is not to sit there and tell people to stop consuming – telling people what they cannot do rarely bears fruit. Design is a needed, necessary and valuable process of invention and innovation, with the potential to take us closer to a sustainable society – a society in which we design *for* sustainable consumption. As a designer, it is unrealistic to think that you will single-handedly save the world, and to pursue this destiny is hazardous, as it sets up an unachievable (utopian) destiny that guarantees failure. Rather, a designer's function is to design in a way that (in practical terms) allows for measured, strategic progress. In this sense, consumption must no longer be polarized in terms of *to consume*, or *not to consume* – particularly when one considers that in the context of design, the model of non-consumption means to design nothing.

Though the designer's role clearly has political impact, designers are not politicians. However, if you embrace consumerism then a role is set up for the designer as a facilitator of objects and experiences that through their existence stimulate and steer real sustainable progress. Furthermore, through *not* consuming, the need for more sustainable products ceases to exist, as if you don't consume, nothing more gets invented and improved. One could understandably respond to this with the cry of 'Good!' Although this is driven by sound intention, the hidden danger is that consumer reality becomes nothing more than an ascetic life sentence, characterized by a noble culture of sacrificial non-enjoyment – not to mention the huge economic transition that this shift implies within a consumer society. The developed and developing worlds are not simply going to stop consuming, and the designer's role becomes clearer the moment we accept this inevitable fact. The aim therefore must be to design in a way that promotes consumption models of long-term sustainability.

While it would be misguided to advocate the mindless, indiscriminate consumption of products, it would be fair to say that there will always be a need for them (as has been proven through millennia of our species *having* and *possessing* material things). So, is designing a recyclable pencil sharpener going to change the world? Perhaps not, but if you strive to accommodate consumer motivation (or lust) with more sustainable products, then improvements are *actually* being made – and there is considerable room for such improvements in today's unsustainable world of goods. Designing in a sustainable way is a proactive engagement with the issues, rather than a fanciful dance within an overly optimistic utopia of non-consumption.

100 per cent sustainable?

Can anything be 100 per cent sustainable? While we still have ice caps, igloos are said to be pretty harmless to the natural world, yet when faced with the everyday demands of commercially driven product design it becomes difficult to imagine how anything manufactured can be *truly* benign in environmental terms. Everything has an impact of some sort, whether through resource extraction, production, shipping, retailing, use, disposal, recycling and so on. So why ask the question? In an etymological sense, sustainability is an 'absolute' term, which implies the total accomplishment of its well-intentioned proposition. In this sense, the sustainability debate should leave little room for discussion. Unfortunately, this approach also adds fuel to the idea that you either *are* or you *ain't* – green or not, sustainable or not. This sweeping overview of reality is grossly unhelpful, as it polarizes what is actually a complex and multifaceted debate. In this way, it can be seen that terminologies such as this are the lowest common denominator where debate is concerned, and unfortunately serve to close down and inhibit discussion, when they should be opening it up and catalysing it.

On the other hand, the idea of 100 per cent sustainability is the ultimate ambition of the sustainable designer; it is the direction we all face, but should do so in the awareness that the term 100 per cent sustainable is as exclusive as it is inclusive. Perhaps a more helpful way of framing this is to consider *degrees of sustainability*. The questions then become: 'How sustainable is it?'; 'How sustainable could it be?'; and 'How can we make it *more* sustainable?' Clearly, new ways of measuring sustainability are greatly needed; ones that are inclusive and participation-widening as a means to engage a broader industry populace. In addition, new means of gauging and mapping sustainability must be more effective in enabling the deeper complexities of the subject to embrace the diversity of creative approaches that might be developed.

In a recent survey staged at the 100 per cent Design exhibition in London (2006), it was found that 53 per cent of those of the design industry that took part in the survey believed that 100 per cent sustainability *is* possible, whereas 47 per cent felt that it was not. The similarity in these opposing results suggests that consensus is far from reached, and sustainable design practice is driven largely by 'perception' as to what is, and what is not effective and achievable. In a field as subjective as design, it is quite understandable that this should be the case. However, these perceptions can become problematic, as they foster the practice of simplistic, symptom-focused paradigms. As such, they tend to incubate popular myths about sustainability, rather than pioneering and adopting a more integrated process that celebrates, through engagement, the complexities and unilateral benefits of a new and creative process that situates sustainability at its centre. It is essential that sustainable design is more than just a box that can be ticked once a recycled material has been specified, or solar cells used, for example. Yes, these changes would make things *more* sustainable, and any motion towards a more sustainable future should be embraced, but that should not, and must not be where the discussion ends. As a discipline, sustainable design requires a level of engagement that must go beyond these immediate solutions, delving deeper into the multifaceted issues relating to object creation, and applying the same level of rigour that would be expected of any other creative discipline. To be effective, sustainable design must become more than a 'bolt-on module' that enables 'conventional design' to transcend its current form. If you want to move closer to the notion of 100 per cent sustainability, you must first embrace the discipline itself, on a deeper level and at the earliest possible opportunity; in doing this, by default, you become a sustainable designer.

Today, we live in a strange time. People often think they are being sustainable when they are not, and the attitude of others – fostered by off-putting doom and gloom diatribes of statistical eco-data that bode the end of the world – is to avoid the issue completely due to the apparent hopelessness of it all. This is a symptom of modern times; when there is ignorance, an oversimplification of sophisticated debates occurs that forces generalizations to be made. Percentages are a mode of description that is often used in a similar context to this. The problem with percentages is that there is no accounting for the complexities of scale. Therefore, it is the journey towards, rather than destination, that industry should be focusing on; thinking in terms of 'ecologies of scale' is helpful in framing this particular scenario – moving from 9 per cent sustainable to 9.5 per cent sustainable is progress after all. For example, if you are a junior designer working with a successful large-scale global brand, your achievement of a 0.5 per cent improvement has a massive impact – particularly when dealing with multiples of millions of units. In contrast to this, the same 0.5 per cent improvement made by a back-bedroom basket-weaver may be less significant in terms of ecological progress, despite their maintaining a healthy eco-persona. Sadly, designers with the potential to make real change often get branded as environmental violators, while less impacting individuals readily receive great applause for achieving relatively little.

Awakening consciousness

For decades now, popular design has eagerly fed the consumer populace with the seemingly infinite stream of *box-fresh* products that they so fervently demand. The culture of consumer-led design is linked with the human desire to express progress, change and development and, in this way, design makes it fashionable to be fashionable; the more we design the new, the more newness is desired and encouraged. However, newness is a transient concept, the unstable character of which, when expressed through products, will always guarantee ultimate disappointment within consumers. Such is the veraciousness of the consumer model and the responsiveness of the ever obliging design industry that the mere passing of time dictates that new gets old, new gets replaced by newer and, within a matter of fleeting moments, version 10.2.1 becomes 10.2.2. Through this persistent inability to satisfy, the cyclic and wasteful model of marketing and design breeds deep 'hunger-pangs' within the consumer psyche. Desire, consumption, waste – followed by re-desire – make up an endless sequence of serial dissatisfaction that represents the ecologically inefficient and destructive process through which we fumble today. Though obscure when described in this way, this treadmill represents a tried and tested economic system that, unfortunately, the globalized industry finds difficult to break away from.

The proliferation of objects that once provided living testimony as to one's degree of individualism and uniqueness is today an ecological burden carried by the entire biosphere, of which we are an integral part. For product designers operating in a mass-consumer context, quantities of product are (by default) commensurate with commercial success, competitive edge and volume, which are often intertwined; just as the premise of 'celebrated design' is so frequently built upon volume, and number of units sold. In this respect, it could be said that resource depletion goes hand-in-hand with global design success. Within this pop-culture design world, creative practitioners often aspire to make the transition from independent designer into a new and high-ranking league of commercial success; local becomes global, batch becomes mass and the bespoke and unknown become 'of-the-moment' household names. In ecological terms, large scale, in itself, is not necessarily a negative force; however, as volume increases, so too does the level of responsibility and burden. So in these scenarios *opportunity knocks* for the sustainable designer: where volume exists, so too do the opportunities for positive change – change that can be acted upon. Too often, sustainable design is served up via exclusive, small-scale and often elite genres of objects. In many respects, bespoke and commission-led design of this nature is not necessarily *the* problem and should in many ways be celebrated, but if this is all that sustainable design is, and can be, then the point is sorely being missed. Sustainable design is essentially about the reduction of impact; therefore, the 'successful' sustainable designer should surely go where 'success' is, where the biggest impacts lie. Sustainable design cannot simply be a marginal activity operating within the safety of a cliquey cell of like-minded greenies. Through the awakened consciousness, sustainable design has acquired a licence to impact upon the mainstream.

Today's demands are being increasingly driven by an awakening consumer consciousness, hungry for more meaningful products boasting a rich and diverse array of tangible eco-credentials, accompanied by a healthy slice of *wearable* ethical status. The more enlightened consumer is now questioning the once celebrated culture of excess that has come to characterize the made world in recent decades. Of course, brands respond to market drivers, and do so readily. However, the collective eco-consciousness of a given multinational corporation will not necessarily be enough to stimulate the degrees of ethical change needed at boardroom level; the driver that ordinarily forces this degree of corporate change is legislation. UK legislation alone provides significant leverage, yet with global market-places, where products are traded internationally, the need for legislation-compliant products is increasing fast. Thus, an enlightened market-place provides an opportunity for capable sustainable designers, while the impact of legislation on multinational industries enables these opportunities to be realized within both commercial and highly competitive contexts. In short, there is an increasing economic demand for sustainable design, driven by both social and governmental change. Happy days!

From theory to practice

So why is it important to engage fully with industry? After all, when one thinks of industry, stereotypically apocalyptic images emerge in the form of the plumes of smoke emanating from chimneys, burning mountains of fossils fuels to turn the 'wheels of industry'. A dystopian image perhaps, but one that is shared by most when faced with the baggage-laden term 'industry'. However, beyond theoretical sustainable design research, it is industry where the decisions are actually made, where ideas are commodified and realized in a physical form, packaged, shipped and sold, where the materials are forged into products. Therefore, to leave industry out of the discussion, or adopt practices that exclude, or even demonize industry's profit-oriented demands, is clumsily to ignore the issue. However, integrating the often conflicting worlds of theory and practice is never a straightforward process. When one considers the tentative adoption of sustainable practices by industry and the lack of integrated and applied sustainable research, it appears obvious that there are unhelpful inhibitors to sustainable progress where it is most needed.

So what is preventing greater conductivity between theory and practice? Theories abound as to why this may be, but it seems obvious that at present the two sides of this debate are not necessarily compatible. In a commercial context shareholder demands tend to ensure that the investment in research is generally driven by an inevitable accountability that has a direct relation to commercial avenues of progression (market research) and, as such, has developed a tendency to be blinkered.

Perhaps due to the seemingly optional nature of increasing the sustainability of one's processes and practices – coupled with the perceived financial and restrictive demands that this might place on economic and creative development – opportunities to invest in sustainable design research are often avoided and dismissed. The commercially oriented system is often incompatible with the non-commercial and scholarly nature of theoretical research, which functions within an entirely different developmental time scale and funding regime. How success is measured in both these fields can differ enormously – in theoretical situations success often relates primarily to originality, and the degree of contribution made to the research field. In addition it tends to exist as a scholarly process that develops relatively freely, due to its independence from day to day constraints of profit-focused industry, and as a result tends to adopt a polarized language that is both remote and inaccessible to the creative industry. The language has thus far failed to penetrate the core of design practice – the one place where it is needed most.

A *carrot and stick* scenario is now emerging where the scissor action of forces of legislation and an increasingly ethically aware market-place are creating an incentive and increasing demand for companies to reconsider their ethical and environmental practices. Taxation poses an economic burden while, in contrast, the weight of demand from an increasingly ethically aware market-place is commercially alluring. This awakening consciousness that can be witnessed across the creative sector is a mere fragment of a broader cultural awakening that is unveiling itself across the world today. This cultural shift is fuelled by a number of contributing factors, from popular media to noticeable changes in weather patterns and the publication of high profile, economically and politically driven research such as the Stern Report.

At first glance this new and enlightened market situation appears wholly positive, and in many respects it is. However, without a considered and informed response to these emergent problems *and* opportunities, we are in danger of turning sustainability into nothing more than a passing trend rather than a deep cultural shift that makes sustainability sustainable. Meanwhile, consumer dizziness grows as marketeers employ increasing magnitudes of ethical spin, with little to follow. This creates an illusion of progress and a false sense of security within consumers and producers, which in many cases places us further away from solutions or meaningful progression. We are experiencing a migration towards more *eco-nomic* opportunities for commercial growth; where ecological concerns are integrated within market demand to create opportunities that offer greater sustainable exchanges between producers, consumers and the environment. Indeed, future success will be measured against sustainability *and* monetary scales. Some more 'forward facing' companies will be quick to take advantage, and succeed in exploiting these new territories, and others will not. In the new *eco-nomic* context the sustainable designer can offer a unique insight and practical capability into new market development rather than simply being employed in a problem solving capacity or to 'pay lip service' to a superficial 'feel-good' agenda. Sustainable design, if situated at the core of change, has the potential to instigate and steer positive *eco-nomic* progress.

About this book

Love it or loath it, design has a central role to play in achieving a sustainable future. Yet despite increased levels of awareness surrounding sustainable design, and how best it may be achieved, it still remains a contentious, apparently complex, bewildering and oftentimes self-contradicting discipline; although contradiction and bewilderment in many respects provide the lifeblood of creative discourse. Healthy debate is essential in working towards sustainability. *Designers, Visionaries and Other Stories* aims to address this by gathering, collating and discussing differing understandings of sustainable design, to curate a comprehensive body of knowledge that widens the participation in sustainable design by reaching beyond the well-intentioned minority (who were already interested in the first place) to more fully engage the broader creative community in the sustainability debate.

    Designers, Visionaries and Other Stories is by key proponents at the forefront of today's sustainable design debate; a book for practitioners of all creative disciplines

– professionals, students and academics. With contributing chapters from Ezio Manzini, John Thackara, Kate Fletcher, Alastair Fuad-Luke, Stuart Walker and John Wood, this challenging book provides the reader with a rich resource of future visions, critical propositions, creative ideas and design strategies for working towards a sustainable tomorrow, today. Among the contributing chapters of this book are further visual contributions, made by members of the creative industry; these images were captured through an information gathering space called '100% Sustainable?', as a feature of the 100% Design exhibition, London, UK (2006). Thirty-eight thousand representatives of the international design industry visiting the show were invited to create a vision, depicting their individual, uncensored perception of sustainable design; dispersed thoughout this book is a small selection of 100 of these visions.

This is not another book about design for recycling, alternative energy or the specification of biodegradable materials. Rather, this book presents pertinent new understandings of sustainable design, to present a challenging, at times uncomfortable and at all times provocative, collection of essays by some of the world's leading sustainable design thinkers. In doing so, this book aims to fuel sustainable design discourse with the rich culture of critique that characterizes effective theory and practice within the creative industry.

The sustainability challenge is a design issue, and as such, this is a book *for* sustainable design, which grows *out* of sustainable design research. Too often, sustainable design practice is unintentionally polarized within either academic or commercial contexts. This provocative text occupies the 'fuzzy' territory between these two worlds, as a means to open the door to designers and researchers alike to enable a greater flow of information between them. Furthermore, the timeliness of this book is underscored by the critical mass of public interest, environmental legislation and design engagement (research and practice). This anthology aims to deepen practical and theoretical understandings of sustainable design through the gathering, collation and mapping of the disparate and isolated bodies of knowledge that have become so characteristic of sustainable design today. In this way, interdisciplinary thinking can be seen to extend theoretical understanding through the connecting of previously disconnected knowledge. Sustainable design is a debate in which fundamental principles, philosophies and working methodologies transcend disciplinary boundaries. In connecting expertise from distinctive corners of the sustainable design field, new insights will emerge that facilitate conceptual understanding – paving the way for positive social, economic and environmental development in a wasteful age of looming ecological crisis, mounting environmental legislation and limited sustainable design progress.

Look at patterns in nature. Networks challenge your world view. Integrate Be prepared to change. Be joyful

sustainability is taking ourself/ourselves seriously as human beings, and recognizing our own best

sustainability is not about global warming and recycling — more — or less — than it is about the responsibility of each and one of us to pursue a more balanced life, a better life and a more meaning-full life for all

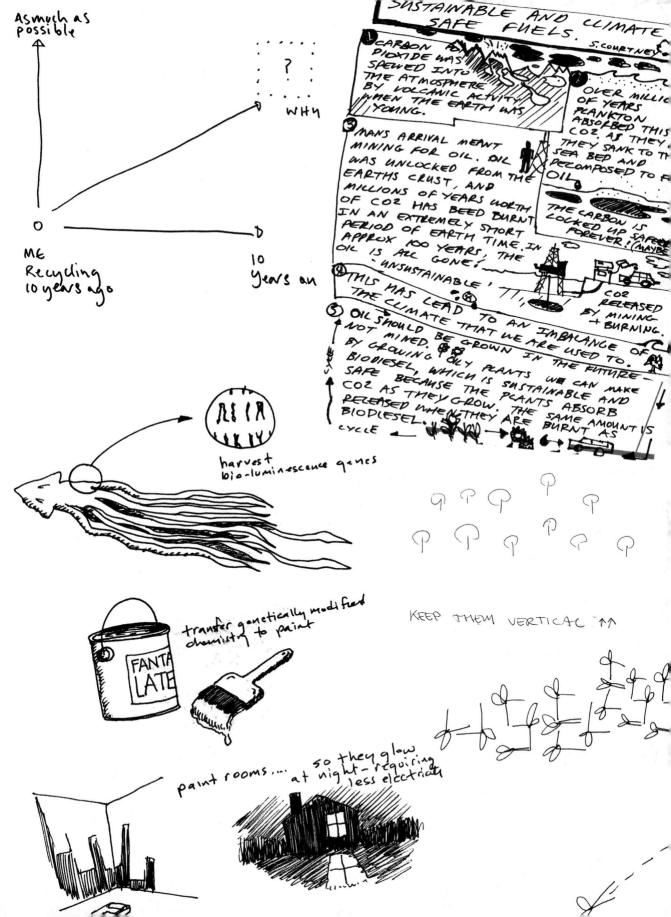

As much as possible

?

WHY

O

ME
Recycling
10 years ago

D

10 Years on

SUSTAINABLE AND CLIMATE SAFE FUELS.
S. COURTNEY

1. CARBON DIOXIDE WAS SPEWED INTO THE ATMOSPHERE BY VOLCANIC ACTIVITY WHEN THE EARTH WAS YOUNG.

2. OVER MILLIONS OF YEARS PLANKTON ABSORBED THIS CO_2. AS THEY SANK TO THE SEA BED AND DECOMPOSED TO FORM OIL.

THE CARBON IS LOCKED UP SAFE FOREVER! (MAYBE)

3. MANS ARRIVAL MEANT MINING FOR OIL. OIL WAS UNLOCKED FROM THE EARTHS CRUST, AND MILLIONS OF YEARS WORTH OF CO_2 HAS BEED BURNT IN AN EXTREMELY SHORT PERIOD OF EARTH TIME. IN APPROX 100 YEARS, THE OIL IS ALL GONE! - UNSUSTAINABLE '.

CO_2 RELEASED BY MINING + BURNING.

4. THIS HAS LEAD TO AN IMBALANCE OF THE CLIMATE THAT WE ARE USED TO.

5. OIL SHOULD BE GROWN IN THE FUTURE - NOT MINED. BY GROWING OILY PLANTS WE CAN MAKE BIODIESEL, WHICH IS SUSTAINABLE AND SAFE BECAUSE THE PLANTS ABSORB CO_2 AS THEY GROW. THE SAME AMOUNT IS RELEASED WHEN THEY ARE BURNT AS BIODIESEL.

CYCLE

harvest
bio-luminescence genes

transfer genetically modified chemistry to paint

FANTA LATE

KEEP THEM VERTICAL ⇑⇑

paint rooms.... so they glow at night - requiring less electricity

Chapter 2

Alastair Fuad-Luke

Re-defining the Purpose of (Sustainable) Design:
Enter the Design Enablers, Catalysts in Co-design

Summary

Advocates of sustainable design have chipped away at defining a new vision for design, by focusing business on the 'triple bottom line' (TBL – the simultaneous pursuit of economic prosperity, environmental quality and social equity). Sadly, their impact has been minimal. Continued economic growth and population increase are negating any gains made by eco-efficient products or services. Design professionals are fluent in 'design for business', but they often have an inadequate grasp of 'design for the environment', and are rarely engaged in 'design for society'. Designers urgently need to move beyond the confines of aesthetic fascism and fetishism tied to the purpose of money making. Design needs a new purpose. Perhaps, on reflection, the real value of design is its *process*. This calls for a new generation of thinking design practitioners willing to help societies to imagine scenarios, encourage participation and maximize collaboration in creating the solutions. Enter the design-enablers, catalysts in designing the future *with*, *for* and *by* society. Co-design creates new outcomes, embues artefacts with new affordances, encourages behavioural change and generates new societal values and enterprise.

Introduction

It may be true that one has to choose between ethics and aesthetics, but whichever one chooses, one will always find the other at the end of the road.

Jean-Luc Godard

The rise of the environmental movement in the 1960s, almost single-handedly catalysed by the author Rachel Carson and her landmark book, *Silent Spring*, gave succour to designers whose world view extended beyond the ethics of business. Early pioneers, such as Richard Buckminster Fuller, Victor Papanek, Christopher Alexander and Ivan Illich, believed that design could, and should, be able to integrate commercial needs with those of society and the environment. Their visions were largely bypassed by successive politico-economic forces in the western world, and the blueprint for a global economy was duly rolled out over the next 30 years. Despite the hiccups of the occasional oil/energy crisis, unemployment and economic recession, continuous growth of gross domestic product (GDP) was the ambition of developed, developing and emerging nations alike. Design gave form to economic ambition. More strictly, design à la mode Raymond Lowey created a chameleon-like aesthetic that embedded the latest technology while simultaneously guaranteeing an early death for artefacts; each generation of artefacts to be conveniently replaced by new 'objects of desire'. At the centre of this web of desire sits the designer, bringing life to objects the very existence of which has been ordained by business strategists, marketeers and economists as 'demanded' by the public. Nigel Whiteley neatly revoked this idea of 'consumer-led' design (Whiteley, 1993), as had Vance Packard some 40 years earlier (Packard, 1957, 1961). Yet the vast majority of designers sign up to the ethics implicit in a business view of the world. Design, its very meaning, its raison d'être, its philosophical core is, today, synonymous with the business of producing, selling and consuming.

The co-dependence of the idea of design with the idea of business has, of course, been contested by designers, though the debate is often dominated by academics rather than practitioners (see, for example, Balcioglu, 1998; Buchanan and Margolin, 1995; European Academy of Design (EAD), 2003). Those who saw design as having responsibilities to the environment and society, as well as business, have challenged the default 'design for business' paradigm. Change in design practice is evident, but it is slow and generally marginalized, so appears unlikely to ferment significant change in the direction or speed of the juggernaut of the global economy. Does this suggest that design needs to review its vision, purpose and sphere of influence? Is this a critical juncture in the history of design? Can design help deliver the societal change necessary to address the complex challenge of creating more sustainable ways of living and working? There are some promising signs that a new way of designing can make a positive contribution – but first an examination of sustainable design progress to date is required.

The limits to growth: Eco-efficiency and business

In the 1990s a trio of landmark books challenged business to change course and embrace ideas of eco-efficiency, an agenda that could satisfy shareholders and meet social responsibilities while reducing environmental impacts (Elkington, 1997; Fussler and James, 1996; Hawkin et al, 1999). The approaches suggested were imaginative and based on a real understanding of the needs of business. Elkington coined the phrase 'triple bottom line' (TBL), defining it as the 'simultaneous pursuit of economic prosperity, environmental quality and social equity'. The TBL model required a shift of current business practices to embrace the concept of sustainable development first given substance by Gro Harlem Bruntland, as 'development that meets the needs of the present without compromising the ability of future generations to meet their own needs' (Bruntland, 1987).

Certain business sectors were galvanized into action and a centre of gravity formed around the eco-efficiency agenda in the form of the World Business Council for Sustainable Development (WBCSD). The WBCSD is an association of global corporates dedicated to finding more environmentally and socially responsible ways of doing business. Charter and Tischner (2001) documented leading edge thinking and practice in the response of the manufacturing and service industries to develop more sustainable solutions. McDonough and Braungart (2002) suggested that a complete rethink was needed in 'the way we make things' and developed the concept of 'triple top line' (TTL), where the objective is to balance economic, social and environmental responsibilities to aim towards a win–win–win situation and focus on 'effectiveness' rather than 'efficiency'.

There are signs that the messaging is hitting home and challenging the culture of business. Over half of the companies listed on the Financial Times Stock Exchange (FTSE) 100 now regularly produce annual reports on their Corporate Social Responsibility (CSR) performance, detailing the positive social contributions and reduced environmental impacts of their businesses. The multinationals have been quick to spot that the ethical investment sector and organic food production/consumption has shown consistent and significant growth in the last decade. A number of well-known ethical brands whose companies were formed in the 1970s have been recently absorbed by multinationals: The Body Shop by L'Oréal; Ben & Jerry's by Unilever; Tom's of Maine by Colgate. British Petroleum (BP) has re-branded itself as a power company, with a weather eye on a post Peak Oil future. Remarkably, even business figureheads are being seen as environmental heroes. Lord John Browne, head of BP, was listed as number 85 in the top 100 green campaigners of all time published by the UK's Environment Agency (Adam, 2006). Twenty-five per cent of the display advertisements in a UK newspaper included reference to eco- or socio-benefits of the companies' products/ services (*The Guardian*, 2006). Not-for-profit organizations, such as the UK's Forum-for-the-Future, celebrate and discourse business progress on the sustainability agenda, detail initiatives from existing companies and promote emerging eco-preneurs. Whether the rhetoric equates to meaningful progress towards more sustainable business is a moot point, but at least positive intentions are being signalled by the business community.

The promise of positive change is there. The reality check is to ask how significant these changes are to business-as-usual? A quick snapshot at global, company and product level is revealing. At a global level the WBCSD currently has about 180 members. The Dow Jones Sustainability Indexes (DJSI), a voluntary and independently vetted system for measuring corporate sustainability and financial performance, has over 320 companies listed, with over half located in Europe.

- There are 320 DJSI members but 5500 members of the mainstream DJ Wilshire RESI and REIT (Total Market) Indexes indicating that only 5.8 per cent of transnational companies have chosen to express their support of sustainability action by joining the DJSI and being independently vetted. Only 1.3 per cent of US companies listed on the DJ Wilshire 5000 Composite Index are DJSI members. Many Fortune 500 companies are not listed on the DJSI.

These data seem to indicate that only the 'early adopters', less than 5 per cent of global corporates, are seriously committed to the TBL and visions of sustainable business.

Even companies with an enlightened attitude to design and sustainability struggle to convince that their overall business model is one that meets long-term sustainability objectives. Philips, the electrical and electronics conglomerate in the Netherlands, has made significant contributions to developing eco-design and life cycle analysis methodologies. Philips list nearly 200 Green Flagship products in their 2005 CSR Report (Philips, 2006). These products represent best eco-design practice, having made significant improvements in at least two of Philips' Green Focal Areas (energy consumption; packaging; hazardous substances; weight; recycling and disposal; lifetime reliability). However, Philips' various divisions (for example, consumer products, lighting, medical equipment) each produce thousands of products, making overall eco-efficiency progress seem rather muted. Couple this with increased sales over recent years and even an enlightened company such as Philips might, in reality, be making little measurable progress in reducing their global environmental footprint.

Finally, at a product level, the eco-efficiency of a product must be viewed in relation to the business system it supports. Belu, a water manufacturer, launched the first 'biodegradable bottle'. Marilyn Smith, Belu co-founder, said: 'Belu's biodegradable bottle is a means of reducing the rubbish in our landfills and empowering consumers to vote for a cleaner planet every time they go in a store' (Design Bulletin, 2006). This seems a welcome innovation bearing in mind that worldwide most water bottles made of polyethylene terepthalate (PET) never enter the recycling stream and end up in landfills or clogging surface water courses or sewage systems. Yet this story neglects the big picture. It doesn't reveal the real energy and environmental costs of the bottle of water in the production and consumption system.

Despite calls for reductions of resource use by 'Factor 4', a concept where natural resources can be used more efficiently by doubling output/wealth and halving resource use (von Weizsäcker et al, 1995), the challenge to business or society to achieve any reduction in per capita material flows is colossal. Thirty tonnes of waste are produced for each tonne of goods reaching the consumer, and 98 per cent of those goods end up being thrown away within six months (Datschefski, 2001). The current *rate* of consumption of global resources in the developed world is equivalent to the 'environmental space' of three planets (MacLaren et al, 1998). With a rapidly expanding consumer middle class in China, India and the 'tiger economies' of SE Asia, and no real slowdown of consumption in the developed world, global per capita consumption appears set to increase not decrease. The complexity of the sustainable consumption agenda, with its heady mix of policy developments, accounting procedures, cognitive psychology ruminations and cultural myths about consumption, seems to suggest this is a societal-wide challenge rather than one where the business of production simply adopts eco-efficiency measures (Jackson, 2006).

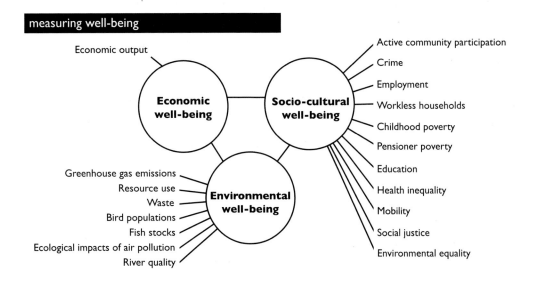

Figure 2.1 The UK government's headline indicators for sustainable development

If the contributions of WBCSD members, Philips or Belu, to sustainable development were measured using the UK government's own headline indicators (Figure 2.1) it is unlikely they would be able really to quantify whether their businesses were making a positive difference other than under the indicator for GDP. Statistics from the UK indicate that decoupling economic growth from resource use and environmental negatives is not happening (Department for Environment, Food and Rural Affairs (Defra), 2004). If businesses were challenged to measure how much well-being they generated through the products they produced using the model developed by Fuad-Luke (2005) (Figure 2.2), it would no doubt generate further head scratching. Herein lies the real challenge to business: can business generate economic well-being while ensuring social fairness and reducing environmental impacts (implying significant resource use reductions)? How can it uncouple business growth from the environmental and social evils? What new models of enterprise

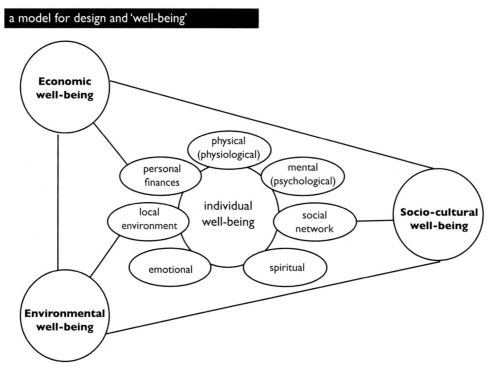

a model for design and 'well-being'

Figure 2.2 A model for design and 'well-being'

Source: adapted from Fuad-Luke, A. (2005) 'A new model of well-being to design 'products' that sustain people, environments and profits', Towards Sustainable Product Design 10, Centre for Sustainable Design, Farnham Castle, Farnham, UK, 24–25 October 2005 might deliver this vision? Lastly, but most importantly, does design have a role in answering these questions?

These questions pose a challenge to the modus operandi of design in the day-to-day politico-economic world. Perceiving design as a generator of well-being offers a framework within which to posit the design challenge of sustainability and a new debate about 'reflective consumption', where 'Design for Reflective Consumption aims to improve people's sense of physiological, psychological, emotional and spiritual well-being, while recognizing issues of economic viability, environmental stability and socio-cultural benefits' (Fuad-Luke, 2005), and well-being is construed as '…a set of context properties which a person perceives to be positive and towards which he steers his action strategy' (Manzini and Jégou, 2003).

Could the creation of well-being, not goods or services, be a new purpose for design?

The problem with design

In the mid 1980s John Elkington was commissioned by the UK Design Council to write a report on green design (Elkington, 1986). He recommended a ten-point checklist (Table 2.1), a common sense approach that could save clients money and produce good design with a smaller environmental footprint. Since then there has been a steady stream of well-researched, accessible, practical and inspirational books on green, eco- and sustainable design for industrial and product designers (for example, Mackenzie, 1990; Whiteley, 1993; Burrall, 1991; Papanek, 1995; Datschefski, 2001; Fuad-Luke, 2002, 2005; Lewis et al, 2001; Ryan, 2004). Despite this plethora of accessible material, penetration of sustainable design practice in the UK is limited, as evidenced by two reports by the Design Council in the last three years (Otto, 2002; Richardson et al, 2005). Sustainability just isn't on the radar screen of the majority of designers. Design professionals are fluent in 'design for business', but they often have an inadequate grasp of 'design for the environment', and are rarely engaged in 'design for society'. The personal statements of 100 'iconic' designers revealed that 1 per cent embed sustainable design thinking (they linked environmental, social and economic factors), 5 per cent occasionally embed eco-design thinking (linking economic and environmental factors), but the vast majority, 94 per cent, focused on other aspects of design (business, production, aesthetics, emotions, innovation, digital).

Table 3.1 Questions for the green designer in the mid 1980s

- Is there a risk of disastrous (environmental and social) failure? i.e. is it likely to cause a catastrophe?
- Could the product be cleaner, i.e. generate less pollution?
- Is it energy-efficient?
- Could it be quieter?
- Should it be more intelligent? i.e. can it monitor and control performance to make it more efficient?
- Is it over-designed? i.e. is it too powerful, wasteful of materials, etc.?
- How long will it last? i.e. can its longevity be extended?
- What happens when its useful life ends? i.e. how is it disposed of, can it be re-used or recycled?
- Could it find an environmental market? i.e. can dangerous materials be transformed into safe, non-toxic materials for new uses?
- Will it appeal to the Green Consumer?

Source: John Elkington Associates (1986) 'Ten questions for the green designer', Design Council, UK

Key barriers to the adoption of sustainable design practice by professionals in the UK (Richardson et al, 2005) are highlighted in Table 2.2. Designers lack skills, hold little influence with decision makers and receive inadequate support from business and government. What could be perceived as a lack of ambition by designers is partially explained by the complex relationship between producers, consumers and designers, with each party unable or unwilling to act on their own. The situation appears further exacerbated by a poor response from design educationalists and higher education institutions to the sustainability agenda.

Table 2.2 Barriers to the adoption of sustainable design practice

Barriers for designers
- Requires larger skill set
- Designers not in influential positions
- Unpopular/misunderstood
- 'Tough sell' to consumers/clients

- Perception of higher cost with respect to sustainable product design (SPD)
- Lack of appropriate tools/methods
- Lack of government support
- Lack of consumer demand

Barriers for corporates (the producers)
- Business case – developing a robust business case that reaches beyond short- term single issues that vie for attention
- Lack of demand – growing markets but still niche/small in terms of market share
- Internalizing external costs – some efficiency gains but often results in net business costs
- Lack of policy incentives – insufficient tax breaks or grants

Barriers for consumers
- Budget targets and cost perceptions: higher prices can exclude sustainable choices; there is a general perception that sustainable products & services are costlier
- Convenience/habit: people are unwilling to change habits and over-estimate the inconvenience of consuming sustainably
- Awareness: people are confused by current information and options and lack trust in information providers

Barriers for design educationalists
- Low level of student demand
- Low level of HE institution interest, understanding and/or perceived importance; therefore little support
- Low level of business demand
- Low level of government support to encourage demand/curriculum change
- Broad and specialist skill set (30 listed skills)
- No or poor track record of graduate employment as sustainable designers
- Lack of stature for design in the market-place
- Sustainability currently not seen as part of mainstream design education
- Lack of appropriate tools/models and/or formal knowledge-sharing network to aid students/practitioners
- Lack of skilled lecturers/tutors
- Lack of entrepreneurial know-how
- SPD requires lifelong learning
- Knowledge exchange network poor beyond specialist individuals and centres
- Poor eco-literacy in school students

To accept these barriers is to accept that those who design must only serve the interests of business. If the real vision is sustainable business then design must treat society and the environment as clients too. This challenges the core notions of design, how it is taught and how it is practised. It immediately focuses discussion on the responsibilities of design and design ethics, topics well covered by leading design thinkers in the early 1990s (see Buchanan and Margolin, 1995, papers by Mitcham, Fry and Manzini) and more recently at the EAD conference on 'design wisdom' (EAD, 2003). It challenges design to deal with its current philosophical crisis (Cooper, 2002), to escape its self-imposed 'cage of aesthetic convention' and find new ways of manufacturing (Walker, 2006). Design, as a profession and a subject field, seems unable or unwilling to take a lead in the challenge of sustainability. Paradoxically, the notion of sustainability offers design its best platform to reinvent itself, to create a new vision and a new purpose.

Revitalizing the idea of design

While everyday manifestations of design often seem bound at the hip to the cycles of fashion and obsolescence and the business ethic, there are many healthy debates challenging the idea of design. These conversations can be construed as a kind of design activism. It seems to focus around various organizations or nodes; for example:

- long established societies (e.g. the Royal Society of the Arts, UK);
- groups or initiatives within government sponsored organizations (e.g. RED, 'Design of the times 2007' (Dott07) at the Design Council, UK);
- not-for-profit foundations (e.g. Eternally Yours Foundation, NL; SlowLab, USA; Positive Alarm, NL; O2, EU; Architecture for Humanity, USA);
- EU funded research projects (Emerging User Demands (EMUDE); Sustainable Everyday, Italy; Attainable Utopias, UK);
- web-zines and blogs (e.g. Designboom, Experientia, Metropolis, Treehugger).

Here there are diverse expressions as to what design has to offer society. These approaches or expressions include open-source design, user-centred design, user-innovation design, service design, metadesign, experience design, empathetic design, inclusive design, universal design, co-design and slow design (Table 2.3). Each approach is a form of design activism that can be posited within a model of sustainable well-being (Fuad-Luke, 2005), although each expression appears to focus on a different set of well-being spheres (Figure 2.3). This loose framework demands questions of the designer as to which approach to apply, and where and how the design will generate well-being. It provides a lens, an approach, through which to view a particular design context. It is not prescriptive but merely sets a potential platform for enquiry. It posits design as the giver of well-being, the change agent from the existing situation to a preferred one (echoing Herbert Simon below). It takes design beyond the prescriptive world of commerce.

Table 2.3 Design activism for a better society

Design activism	Definition	Sources
Open-source design	Open design is the investigation and potential of open source and the collaborative nature of the internet to create physical objects. People apply their skills and time to projects for the common good, perhaps where funding or commercial interest is lacking.	Wikipedia, Nov 2006
User-centred design	UCD is a design philosophy and a process in which the needs, wants and limitations of the end user of an interface or document are given extensive attention at each stage of the design process.	Wikipedia, Nov 2006
	UCD describes design, based on the needs of the user.	Norman, D. A. (1986) *The Psychology of Everyday Things*
	Fundamental to user-centred design is that the best-designed products and services result from understanding the needs of the people who will use them.	Black, A., The Design Council, Nov 2006
Service design	Service design can be both tangible and intangible. It can involve artefacts as well as communication, environment and behaviours. Service design is the specification and construction of technologically networked social practices that deliver valuable capacities for action to a particular customer.	Wikipedia and The Design Council, Nov 2006

Metadesign	Metadesign is an emerging conceptual framework aimed at defining and creating social and technical infrastructures in which new forms of collaborative design can take place. Metadesign extends the traditional notion of design beyond the original development of a system to include *co-adaptive processes* between users and systems, which enable the users to act *as designers and be creative.*	Giaccardi, E. and Fischer, G. (2005) 'Creativity and evolution: A metadesign perspective', in 6th International Conference of the EAD (AD06) on Design>System>Evolution, Bremen, University of the Arts, 29–31 March 2005
Experience design	Experience design is the practice of designing products, processes, services, events and environments – each of which is a human experience – based on the consideration of an individual's or group's needs or desires, beliefs, knowledge, skills, experiences and perceptions.	Wikipedia, Nov 2006
	Experience design strives to create experiences beyond products and services. Its boundaries go beyond traditional design.	AIGA Experience Design, Nov 2006
	Experience design is driven by consideration of the 'moments' of engagement between people and brands, and the memories these create.	Ardil, R., The Design Council, Nov 2006
Empathetic design	'Empathetic design practice is about combining these subjective approaches …[empathy, intuition, inspiration and subjective visions are ambiguous] with user data and other sources of objective information.'	Black, A. (1998) 'Empathetic design: User focused strategies for innovation', in proc. of New Product Devt., IBC Conferences, quoted by Mattelmaki, T. (2003) 'Probes: Studying experiences for design empathy', in Koskinen et al, *Empathetic Design – User Experiences in Product Design*, IT Press, Helsinki, pp119–130

Inclusive/ universal design	Inclusive design is about ensuring that environments, products, services and interfaces work for people of all ages and abilities.	Helen Hamlyn Research Institute, Nov 2006
	Inclusive design is a process whereby designers, manufacturers and service providers ensure that their products and services address the needs of the widest possible audience.	DTI (2000) Foresight programme, Dept of Trade & Industry, London
	Universal design is an approach to the design of products, services and environments to be usable by as many people as possible regardless of age, ability or situation.	Wikipedia, Nov 2006
Co-design, co-creation, participatory design, collaborative design, cooperative design, transformation design	Participatory design (PD) is a design framework and related methods which advocate user involvement in design, and a political stance advocating worker rights.	Axup, Jeff – Mobile Community Design blog, Nov 2006
	Participatory design … a term that refers to a large collection of attitudes and techniques predicated on the concept that the people who ultimately will use a designed artefact are entitled to have a voice in determining how the artefact is designed.	Carroll, John M. 'Dimensions of participation in Simon's design', *Design Issues*, vol 22, no 2, pp3–18, Spring 2006, MIT
Slow design	Slow design is 'design to slow metabolisms (economic, resource flows, human) and to celebrate slowness as a counterbalance to the 'fastness' or speed of the current design paradigm'.	Fuad-Luke (2002) and www.slowdesign.org, Nov 2006
	The ethos of slow design is to encourage human flourishing (*eudaimonia*, Greek) within a meta-paradigm of a socially equable world, a regenerative environment, and renewed visions of living and enterprise.	Fuad-Luke (in press) and www.slowlab.net, Jan 2006

Figure 2.3 Design activist approaches and their primary focal points in a model of well-being

(*Key*: Grey spheres of well-being are a primary focal point, white spheres of well-being are secondary focal points)

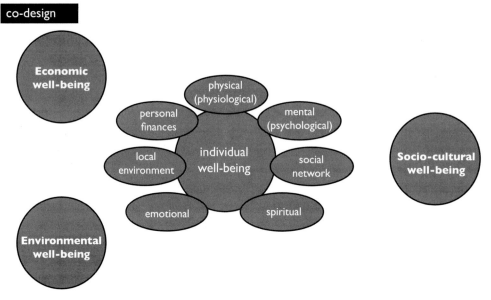

Figure 2.3a The desired design model for 'co-design'

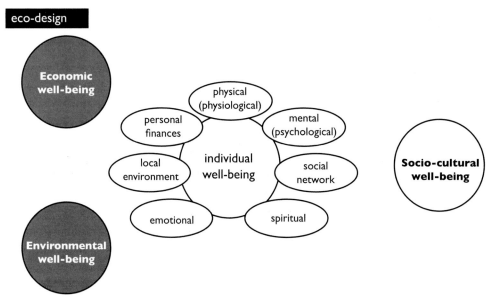

Figure 2.3b The current model for eco-design of efficient products/services

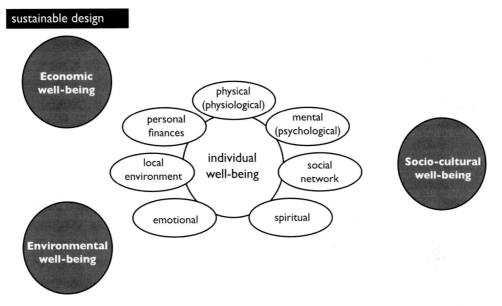

Figure 2.3c The current model for sustainable product design (SPD)

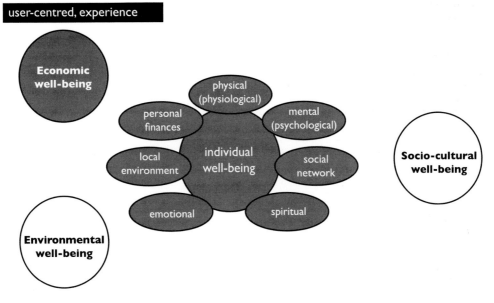

Figure 2.3d The current model for user-centred design

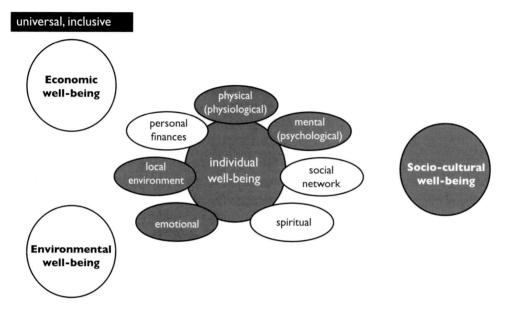

Figure 2.3e The current model for universal or inclusive design

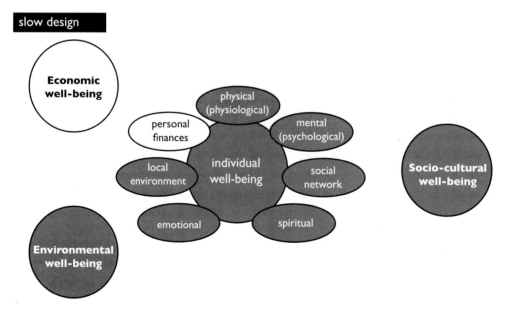

Figure 2.3f The current model for 'slow design'

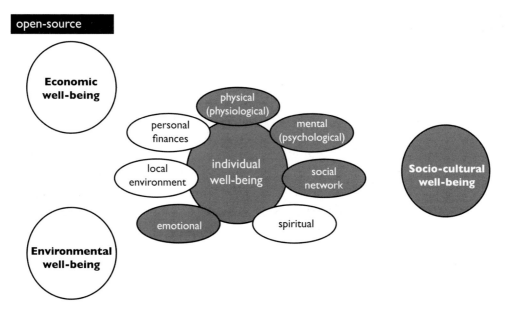

Figure 2.3g The current model for 'open-source' design

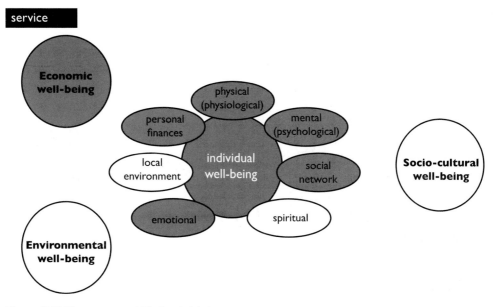

Figure 2.3h The current model for 'service' design

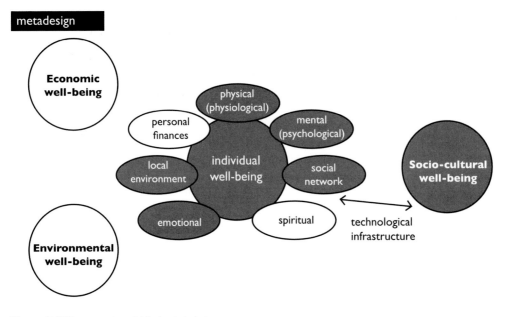

Figure 2.3i The current model for 'metadesign'

Designing together

Being a noun and a verb, 'design' has many mutable meanings, but in common parlance it is firmly owned by the hegemony of commercial brands geared to *unsustainable* consumption. Simply put, design *is* business. Even eco-efficient design is business too. The medium- and long-term sustainability of eco-efficient design depends upon the ecological rucksack and footprint of each 'design' (product, service, building, etc.), the resource flows/availability, the ability of the environment to absorb the inputs/outputs associated with the 'design', and the size of the human population demanding the 'design'. Design is so strongly associated with the idea of commercial manufacturing and building that we have forgotten the real importance of design.

Herbert Simon's broad definition of design, 'Everyone designs to move from existing situations into preferred situations' (Simon, 1996), enables diverse meanings and interpretations of design to emerge. These include everything from the humble everyday ritual of designing one's breakfast to the design of products or the design institutions or organizations that catalyse 'trigger points' (radical societal shifts). It is this looser, yet more accessible definition of design that might point the way forward for a renewed purpose for design. It implies that *changing is also designing*. Change is implicit in the journey towards more sustainable ways of producing and consuming, as it is any exercise that involves cultural behavioural change. It also necessitates a shift in how we measure well-being, how we define economic progress, and how we want societies to develop. In short, sustainability demands a re-evaluation of societal values at global, regional, national and local levels. This way of designing can not be confined to the work of specialists (designers with some kind of formal training) but is, by necessity, *design with, for and by society*.

Design WITH, FOR and BY society

Fundamentally, sustainability cannot be achieved if only particular individuals or sectors of society see it as an ambition. Sustainability has to be a cooperative ambition, a societal ambition. It requires that society has a universal awareness of its condition before taking the radical steps on the sustainability road. Recent mediation of the climate change debate in the UK and USA has raised that universal awareness (or for those who remember the environmental and energy crisis of the 1970s, revived that universal awareness). Certainly the recent publication of the Stern Review (Stern, 2006) and Al Gore's film *An Inconvenient Truth*, plus the attendant publicity they received, might be perceived as a watershed and a potential catalyst in shifting socio-political and economic thinking. Stern's suggestion that immediate remedies to halt or slow climate change might cost 1 per cent of world GDP today, but a laggard response could end up *decreasing* world GDP by 5–20 per cent, might engender a critical shift in attitudes and stimulate actions. The costs of climate change, coupled with the prospect of a post Peak Oil future, are capturing the attention of the politicians and the populace alike.

Are there precedents during the era of the consumer economy for a more society-oriented way of designing? Yes, 'participatory design' has its roots in the labour movements in Scandinavia in the 1950s. Furthermore, the terminology has diversified since then to embrace 'collaborative design', 'cooperative design', 'co-design' and 'social design' (Margolin and Margolin, 2002). More recently, co-design has been renamed 'transformation design' by the RED group at the UK Design Council (Burns et al, 2006).

The terms 'participatory' or 'co-design' seem particularly useful as they are self explanatory. The essence of co-design is that it is an approach 'predicated on the concept that people who ultimately use a designed artifact are entitled to have a voice in determining how the artifact is designed' (Carroll, 2006).

There are several core principles. Co-design is not a single procedure or ingredient. It is a commitment regarding power and inclusion. Co-design involves *mutual learning* in a multi-stakeholder environment. Co-design invokes many of the characteristics of soft system methodologies, as described in Broadbent (2003):

- being a holistic, intuitive, descriptive, experiential and empirical, pragmatic and wisdom/values-based approach;
- being an iterative, non-linear, interactive process;
- being 'action-based' research;
- involving 'top-down' and 'bottom-up' approaches;
- simulating the real world;
- being useful for complex systems or problems;
- being situation driven, especially by common human situations;
- satisfying pluralistic outcomes;
- being internalized by the system.

The more commercially oriented aspects of co-design are also manifest in a variety of user-centred or user-innovation design approaches, although the main goal is the production of profitable, rather than sustainable, goods and services. For example, Philips has just entered the virtual world Second Life in order to explore the potentiality of 'crowdsourcing' in product development. Fiat recently used a web blog to engage customers in design of the new Fiat Bravo car.

The internet provides an infrastructure for social and collaborative networking that engenders co-design, especially in open-source environments. The growth of online resources from Wikipedia (information), YouTube (entertainment) to the BBC's Climate Change Experiment attests to the potential power of internet collaboration.

Co-design in action

Co-design challenges how we use design to grow, nurture and sustain human, social, financial and environmental capital. Co-design's remit is not confined to aesthetics, technology, form and profit. Implicit in the very act of co-design is the choreography of the aforementioned 'capitals' *and* the (re)design of enterprises, institutions and organizations, be they commercial, not-for-profit, community or governmental. In this sense co-design sees its role as central to the organization of enterprise, as expressed in Peter James' model (James, 2001) (Figure 2.4), as well as the form-making of artefacts. Co-design sees everyone as designers, yet simultaneously recognizes the catalytic power of strategic designers, design managers, product designers, engineers, architects and other recognized design disciplines.

   Co-design embraces multi-stakeholder involvement, where the stakeholders-as-designers, and the designers themselves, learn and create together. There's no blueprint for a way of co-designing, but involvement by the stakeholders is a key feature. Many working in the voluntary and charitable sectors or those involved in social enterprises might recognize the spirit and process of co-design. The examples selected below illustrate the 'added-value' that designers can bring to a co-design project. The 'client' in these co-design projects seems to embrace the man-made world (society, business, technology, etc.) and the natural world. Co-design tries to balance anthropocentric, social and humanist concerns with a lighter ecological footprint.

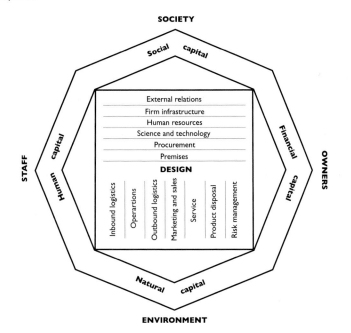

Figure 2.4 Design – at the centre of an organization

Source: James, P. (2001) 'Towards sustainable business?' in Charter, M. and Tischner, U. (eds) *Sustainable Solutions*, Greenleaf Publishing, Sheffield; adapted from Porter (1985, p37)

1 Architecture

Rural Studio, set up by the architect Samuel Mockbee, has offered a generation of architectural students in the University of Auburn University, southern USA, a chance to create, design, build, redesign and rebuild the homes of poor Americans. Students sometimes stay with their hosts to learn about each unique design context, the final design being born of an intimate knowledge of people, place and local materials. Designs seek the needs of local people and communities from within the communities' context.

Architecture for Humanity (AFH). Founded in 1999 by Cameron Sinclair, this not-for-profit enterprise co-creates temporary/permanent designs and housing to deal with global, social and humanitarian crises. AFH believes 'that where resources and expertise are scarce, innovative, sustainable and collaborative design can make a difference'. Its design ethos is 'co-creation' with an emphasis on facilitation, enablement and empowerment rather than dependency.

2 Urban services

Sustainable Everyday and EMUDE. These two projects were funded by the Sixth Environment Programme of the European Union, coordinated by the design department at Milan Polytechnic. Sustainable Everyday coordinated the efforts of 15 design schools from around the globe to create scenarios for product service systems (PSS), or services that would reduce environmental load and increase social benefits (Manzini and Jégou, 2003). Their approach was to create design scenarios that provided access to 'functionings' and encouraged people to extend their 'capability', with a view to raising people's 'well-being'. EMUDE examined hundreds of successful European community or social enterprise projects revealing promising social innovation in terms of sustainable development. Many projects embrace multi-stakeholders and have knowingly or unknowingly used a 'bottom-up' co-design approach.

The Green Map System. Founded in 1995, Green Maps is a locally adaptable, globally shared framework for environmental mapmaking. Mapping local urban or rural communities, using a generic and adaptable visual language based on icons, mapmakers show where green shops, sites and cultural resources are located. This is a global system of 276 maps representing most of the world's capital cities and specific localities. It represents a robust marriage of an open-source information system that embeds local adaptability within a recognized brand. Each map is an idiosyncratic mirror of the locality.

3 Food

Slow Food was founded by Carlo Petrini in 1986 in Italy to promote food and wine culture and defend food and agricultural diversity worldwide. The Slow Food Foundation for Biodiversity points out that since 1900 there has been a loss of 75 per cent of European and 93 per cent of USA food diversity. Approximately 30,000 vegetable varieties became extinct in the last century. Over 20 years, Slow Food has attracted 83,000 members in 800 *convivia* in 50 countries and 400 *condotte* in Italy. Local convivia are given autonomy to design their own organizations but get support from Slow Food to maintain a global profile and impact. Slow Food has consistently raised the importance of localization of food production for socio-cultural well-being and sustainability.

4 Schools

Walking Bus is a powerful antidote to the complex, interconnected problems of obesity, children's health, mobility choices for home to school transportation, and education. The concept is strikingly simple. Each walking bus has an adult 'driver' at the front and an adult 'conductor' at the back. The children walk to school along a pre-planned route picking up additional 'passengers' at specific 'bus-stops'. Each walking bus is 'designed' to meet the needs of local stakeholders, which include the school children, parents, bus volunteers, the schools, road traffic and safety managers, and local authorities.

Growing Schools is a UK initiative involving 15,000 schools. It is supported by a website that shows how teachers and children can create gardens in the school grounds to provide an 'outdoor classroom'. Extensive resources inspire lesson plans, schemes of work, curriculum support and learning materials with the potent reality of designing and making a garden. The scheme embraces everything from 'grow your own potatoes competition' to lessons in climate change in your own living laboratory.

5 Re-manufacturing

The SOFA Project, Bristol, is one of the UK's leading re-use charities providing low-cost furniture and appliances to people living on low incomes. Established in 1980, it now helps furnish 7000 homes annually with affordable furniture and appliances for low income families. In doing so it re-uses 1.5 million items of furniture and diverts 63,000 tonnes of waste from landfill. It is a member of the Furniture Re-use Network (FRN) involving over 300 UK community organizations. Work and training placements for the unemployed and socially excluded provide service to local communities and individuals.

Can co-design be applied to commercial projects?

The design of any project where the multi-stakeholders are engaged by the designers in a co-design process has the potentiality to create fresh solutions. A demonstration of this is seen in an ongoing project by 3bornes ARCHITECTES commissioned to design a new municipal kitchen (Figure 2.5). Besançon is the capital and provincial city of the Franche-Comté region of north-eastern France, with a population of 220,000. Reknowned for its microtechnology and watch-making businesses, the town has an illustrious architectural and military history. The central kitchen, La Cuisine Centrale de Besançon, serves 5500 meals daily for 80 schools in the town.

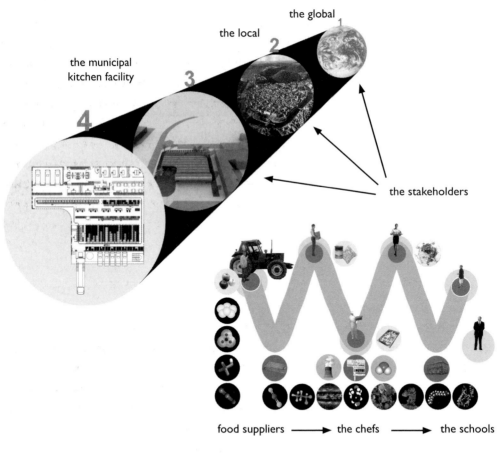

Figure 2.5 Co-design in action: A kitchen for schools in the town of Besançon, eastern France (La Cuisine Centrale de Besançon)

3bornes ARCHITECTES won the commission in June 2006 from the local authority in Besançon to develop a new kitchen facility. Francois Tesnière and Anne-Charlotte Goût, the founders of 3borne ARCHITECTES, brought technical and other design experts together to form a team premised on the idea of co-design. Through the inspiration of Tesnière the team encouraged participation from external upstream and downstream stakeholders with the authority's own departments (technical services, education, logistics) and employees (cooks, waste managers). Stakeholders were encouraged to examine the design of the building using the principles of sustainability – minimum environmental impact, maximum social benefits and best-fit financial viability (capital and operational costs) – by running workshops and through the use of questionnaires. Concepts such as a low carbon footprint meal were used to engage the stakeholders in a basket of issues from 'food miles' to local organic food production to nutritional requirements, cooking equipment, energy supply and energy security. Workshop participants were asked to create scenarios to examine alternative design possibilities. By examining these issues in an environment of discourse the stakeholders were engaged with a new sense of responsibility beyond the mere construction of a municipal food kitchen. For example, a roof garden was proposed as a bioclimatic building measure and as a multi-stakeholder meeting space, where food suppliers, the cooks, parents, teachers and the schoolchildren could get together. Here was the potential for dialogue about the design of future meals and recipes and the development of systems to encourage the supply of more local/regional foods into the supply chain.

Working with the chefs, the innovative 2zones2 system (an eco-designed system of ergonomic and hygienic workflows of raw, fragilized and finished food) was configured to meet the needs of the cooks while simultaneously challenging their current way of working. The workshops encouraged participation within the budgetary constraints to get the 'best fit' solution.

The co-design approach permitted the client and stakeholders to see macro- and micro-perspectives in developing a *food system*, rather than just a kitchen. Co-design embeds latent potentiality into the form making (a new kitchen building and facilities) to make a holistic contribution to education, local food supply, regional food identity and more.

New ways of designing and making

The challenge of sustainability is an *opportunity* to design new enterprises or redesign existing enterprises. Potentially these enterprises can ensure they provide gainful and fair employment, now and for future generations, while minimizing environmental impacts and/or maintaining or restoring environmental/ecological capacity. The evidence of this opportunity is a raft of eco-entrepreneurial companies that simply didn't exist a few years ago. Take for example Ecover, the Belgian household detergent and cleaner manufacturer; Freeplay, the European wind-up radio manufacturers; Kopf, the German solar-power boat makers; Smile Plastics, the UK recycled sheet plastic manufacturer; Second Nature, manufacturers of sheep's wool building insulation; and Smart Cars, originally a joint venture between Swatch and Mercedes-Benz, now owned by DaimlerChrysler. And there are hundreds of companies that see a robust future for eco-efficient products (see for example, Datschefski, 2001; Fuad-Luke, 2005).

Can future eco-enterprises be more radical, deliver more social good, and further reduce environmental impacts? Undoubtedly yes, especially if the formation of new social enterprises (enterprises with socially and/or environmentally oriented goals) is encouraged by government. Certainly, the Social Enterprise Unit within the UK DTI is supporting new social enterprise ventures, as they often generate strong local community or environment benefits. Walker (2006) makes a cogent case for rethinking our systems of manufacturing to permit serial and sequential upgrade of components to create more meaningful, emotional and durable relationships between the user and the product. Such systems would involve a radical rethink of the underlying business models currently associated with mass manufacturing. Fuad-Luke (2007, in press) suggests several avenues of exploration for future making (Figures 2.6a and b). The first is the balance between how much is actually made and finished by the manufacturer and how much is 'made' and 'finished' or customized/personalized by the user. How much is designed professionally and how much by the user? The second is whether we individually or collectively own artefacts or whether we rent/lease/buy services. This agenda has been extensively explored in the debate around product service systems in the recently completed SusProNet project, now embraced by a new European project on sustainable production and consumption called SCORE.

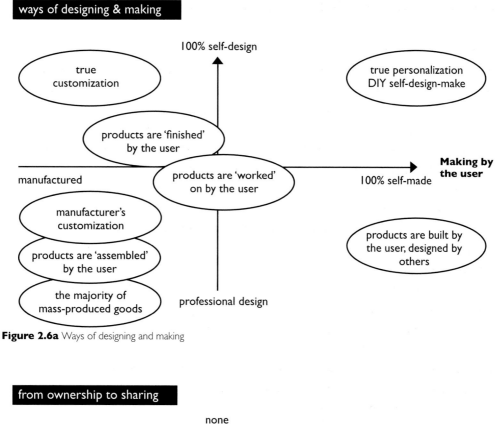

Figure 2.6a Ways of designing and making

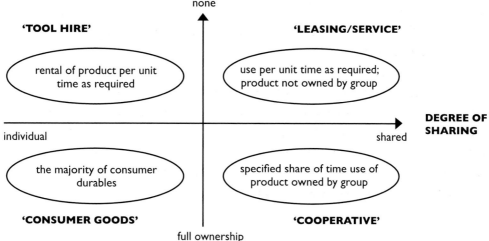

Figure 2.6b From ownership to sharing

Co-designing new affordances, new values

Co-design is a design collaboration involving diverse stakeholders; it is therefore characterized as being societal rather than just commercial. The co-design approach or philosophy seems well placed to answer a question raised by John Wood: 'Could design bring human society closer to an attainable form of utopia?' (Wood, 2003). Wood argued that design 'could be considered as the wise regulation of dynamic elements such as flow, integration, awareness and value' (Figure 2.7). The default design paradigm is really the business-as-usual paradigm (see for example, Findeli 2001), so the dynamics and the effects of design activities are largely regulated by business. The affordances[1] of designs made by business do not necessarily represent the affordances of designs configured by societal forces. Co-design offers potentiality to generate new ideas of meeting our (sustainability) well-being needs. It can achieve this by:

- improving participation and communication;
- fostering co-existence;
- catalysing conviviality;
- generating new affordances.

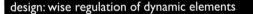

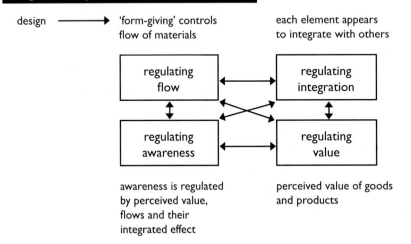

Figure 2.7 John Wood's design arena

Source: Adapted from Wood, J. (2003) 'The wisdom of nature = The nature of wisdom. Could design bring human society closer to an attainable form of utopia?' Paper presented at 5th European Design Academy conference, 28–30 April 2003, Barcelona

In doing so, co-design has the potentiality to establish new memes[2] and genres of form that embed ideas of sustainability.

Co-design challenges the current (default) binary designer-client based ethical code. It suggests that the 'client' is society at large. Co-design might therefore benefit from an ethical framework along the lines of the Hippocratic oath taken by medical practitioners. Co-designers are concerned with the well-being and health of society and the environment over and above purely commercial interests.

Co-design requires designers to foster new skills. Designers must become or improve their abilities as enablers, catalysts, activists, facilitators, connectors, arbitrators, storytellers, visualizers and scenario setters. Designers might aspire to:

- design intelligence (Fry, Tony, date unknown);
- design mindfulness (Findeli, 2001);
- design thinking (MacDonald 2001);
- design hermeneutics (interpretations) (Willis, 1999);
- design persuasiveness (Willis, 1999);
- design virtues (Bonsiepe, 1998);
- design pluralism (Fuad-Luke, 2002, 2005);
- design functionings and capabilities (Manzini and Jégou, 2003).

Co-design demands sensitivities well beyond the palette of design activities associated with the materialization of form for the purpose of business. It is for this reason that co-design offers a fundamental new purpose for (sustainable) design. That purpose is design to enable societies to design their own futures based on equity (intra- and intergenerational, between poor and rich, between ethnic and racial groups), human flourishing, and long-term environmental diversity and stability. Design's focus in the 'age of sustainability' should be well-being, not stuff, things, goods. Designers, from laypeople to professionals, can become the conduits, the shamans of society, linking society to a viewpoint beyond anthropocentrism. The purpose of (co-)design is the creation of new societal values to balance human happiness with ecological truths. In doing so, design contests the notion of material and economic progress, and its inherent ecological untruths.

Notes

1   J.J. Gibson defined 'affordance' as the notion that forms or configurations offer possibilities, availabilities, actions or conveniences to us.

2   'Memes' are self-replicating physical or non-physical things that contribute to the process of evolution. Memes operate in biotic or abiotic environments, in anthropocentric or biocentric world views. Memes can be patterns, habits, jokes, fashions, myths. The notion of 'sustainability' has currency as a meme but like all anthropocentric memes its currency varies across societies and cultures. 'Walking Bus' is a real service and a meme.

References

Adam, D. (2006) 'Earthshakers: The top 100 green campaigners of all time', *The Guardian*, Tuesday 26 November, pp8–9

Balcioglu, T. (ed) (1998) *The Role of Product Design in Post-Industrial Society*, Kent Institute of Art & Design, Kent, and Middle East Technical University Faculty of Architecture Press, Ankara

Black, A. (1998) 'Empathetic design: User focused strategies for innovation', in proc. of New Product Devt., IBC Conferences, quoted by Mattelmaki, T. (2003) 'Probes: Studying experiences for design empathy', in Koskinen et al, *Empathetic Design – User Experiences in Product Design*, IT Press, Helsinki, pp119–130

Bonsiepe, G. (1998) 'Some virtues of design', a contribution to the symposium, 'Design beyond Design…' in honour of Jan van Toom, held at the Jan van Eyck Academy, Maastricht, November 1997, published 2 November 1998

Broadbent, J. (2003) 'Generations in design methodology', *The Design Journal*, vol 6, no 1, pp2–13

Bruntland, G. (ed) (1987) *Our Common Future: The World Commission on Environment and Development*, Oxford University Press, Oxford

Buchanan, R. and Margolin, V. (eds) (1995) *Discovering Design – Explorations in Design Studies*, The University of Chicago Press, Chicago and London, pp173–243

Burns, C., Cottam, H., Vanstone, C. and Winhall, J. (2006) 'Transformation design', RED Paper 02, February, The Design Council, London, www.designcouncil.org.uk/RED/transformationdesign, accessed November 2006

Burrall, P. (1991) *Green Design*, Issues in Design, The Design Council, London

Carroll, J. M. (2006) 'Dimensions of participation in Simon's design', *Design Issues*, vol 22, no 2, pp3–18, Spring, MIT

Carson, R. (1962) *Silent Spring*, Houghton Mifflin, Boston, MA

Charter, M. and Tischner, U. (eds) (2001) *Sustainable Solutions: Developing Products and Services for the Future*, Greenleaf Publishing, Sheffield

Cooper, R. (2002) 'Design: Not just a pretty face', *The Design Journal*, vol 5, no 3, pp1–2

Datschefski, E. (2001) *The Total Beauty of Sustainable Products*, Rotovision, Hove

Defra (2004) 'Sustainable development indicators in your pocket', a selection of the UK government's indicators of sustainable development, National Statistics/Defra, Defra Publications, London

Elkington, J. (1997) *Cannibals with Forks: The Triple Bottom Line of 21st Century Business*, Capstone Publishing, Oxford

European Academy of Design (2003) The 5th EAD conference, 'Design Wisdom', Barcelona, 28–30 April, www.ub.es/5ead, accessed December 2006

Fiell, C. and Fiell, P. (2001) *Designing the 21st Century*, Taschen, Cologne

Findeli, A. (2001) 'Rethinking design education for the 21st century: Theoretical, methodological and ethical discussion', *Design Issues*, vol 17, no 1, Winter, pp5–17

Fuad-Luke, A. (2002, 2005) *The Eco-design Handbook*, Thames & Hudson, London

Fuad-Luke, A. (2005) 'A new model of well-being to design "products" that sustain people, environments *and* profits', in Towards Sustainable Product Design 10, Centre for Sustainable Design, Farnham Castle, Farnham, 24–25 October

Fuad-Luke, A. (2007, in press) 'Adjusting our metabolism: Slowness and nourishing rituals of delay in anticipation of a Post-Consumer Age', in T. Cooper (ed) *Longer Lasting Solutions: Advancing Sustainable Development Through Increased Product Durability*, Gower Publishing, London

Fussler, C. and James, P. (1996) *Driving Eco-innovation*, Pitman Publishing, London

Giaccardi, E. and Fischer, G. (2005) 'Creativity and evolution: A metadesign perspective', in 6th International Conference of the EAD (AD06) on Design>System>Evolution, Bremen, University of the Arts, 29–31 March 2005

Hawkin, P., Lovins, A. B. and Lovins, L. H. (1999) *Natural Capitalism: The Next Industrial Revolution*, Earthscan, London

Jackson, T. (ed) (2006) *The Earthscan Reader in Sustainable Consumption*, Earthscan, London

James, P. (2001) 'Towards sustainable business?', in M. Charter and U. Tischner (eds) *Sustainable Solutions: Developing Products and Services for the Future*, Greenleaf Publishing, Sheffield, pp77–97

John Elkington Associates (1986) 'Ten questions for the green designer', a report for The Design Council, London

Lewis, H., Gertsakis, J., Grant, T., Morelli, N. and Sweatman, A. (2001) *Design + Environment: A Global Guide to Designing Greener Goods*, Greenleaf Publishing, Sheffield

MacDonald, N. (2001) 'Can designers save the world? (and should they try?)', *newdesign*, September/October, pp29–33

McDonough, W. and Braungart, M. (2002) *Cradle to Cradle: Remaking the Way We Make Things*, North Point Press, New York

Mackenzie, D. (1990) *Green Design: Design for the Environment*, Lawrence King Publishing, London

MacLaren, D., Bullock, S. and Yousuf, N. (1998) *Tomorrow's World. Britain's Share in a Sustainable Future*, Friends of the Earth/Earthscan, London

Manzini, E. and Jégou, F. (2003) *Sustainable Everyday: Scenarios of Urban Life*, Edizioni Ambiente, Milan

Margolin, V. and Margolin, S. (2002) 'A "social model" of design: Issues of practice and research, *Design Issues*, vol 18, no 4, Autumn, pp24–30

Norman, D. A. (1986) *The Psychology of Everyday Things*, Basic Books, New York

Otto, B. (2002) 'Searching for solutions, A report for the Design Council', July 2002, Design Council, London

Packard, V. (1957) *The Hidden Persuaders*, Penguin, Harmondsworth

Packard, V. (1961) *The Waste Makers*, Penguin, Harmondsworth

Papanek, V. (1995) *The Green Imperative: Natural Design for the Real World*, Thames & Hudson, London

Philips (2006) 'Creating value', Sustainability Report 2005, Philips Corporate Sustainability Office, Eindhoven, www.philips.com/assets/Downloadablefile//SAR2005_screen-15318.pdf, accessed January 2007

RED, Design Council, see Burns et al (2006)

Richardson, J., Irwin, T. and Sherwin, C. (2005) 'Design & sustainability', a scoping report for the Sustainable Design Forum, published by The Design Council, 27 June

Ryan, C. (2004) *Digital Eco-Sense: Sustainability and ICT – A New Terrain for Innovation*, lab.3000, Victoria

Simon, H. A. (1996) *Sciences of the Artificial*, 3rd rev edn, The MIT Press, Cambridge, MA

Stern, N. (2006) *The Economics of Climate Change*, The Stern Review, Cabinet Office – HM Treasury, Cambridge University Press, Cambridge

The Guardian (2006) Guardian Media Group, 25 June

Walker, S. (2006) *Sustainable by Design: Explorations in Theory and Practice*, Earthscan, London

von Weizsäcker, E. U., Lovins, A. and Lovins, H. (1995) *Factor 4: Doubling Wealth – Halving Resource Use*, Earthscan, London

Whiteley, N. (1993) *Design for Society*, Reaktion Books, London

Willis, A.-M. (1999) 'Ontological designing', paper presented at the 3rd EAD conference, 'Design Cultures', at Sheffield Hallam University, Sheffield, May

Wood, J. (2003) 'The wisdom of nature = the nature of wisdom. Could design bring human society closer to an attainable form of utopia?', paper presented at the 5th EAD conference, 'Design Wisdom', Barcelona, 28–30 April, www.ub.es/5ead/PDF/8/Word.pdf, accessed December 2006

Organizations and their web sites

2zones2, www.2zones2.com/, January 2007

3bornesARCHITECTES, www.3bornes.com/, January 2007

AIGA Experience Design. www.aiga.org, November 2006

Architecture for Humanity, www.architectureforhumanity.org/about/aboutus.html, January 2007

Attainable Utopias, www.attainable-utopias.org/ds21, January 2007

BBC Climate Change Experiment, www.bbc.cpdn.org, January 2007

Design Bulletin, www.brandrepublic.com, February 2006

Design Council, www.designcouncil.org.uk, November 2006, January 2007

Dow Jones Sustainability Indexes, www.sustainability-indexes.com, January 2007

DTI, Department of Trade and Industry, www.dti.gov.uk, 2000

EMUDE, www.sustainable-everyday.net/EMUDE, January 2007

Eternally Yours Foundation, www.eternally-yours.nl, February 2007

Experientia blog, www.experientia.com/blog, January 2007

Forum for the Future, www.forumforthefuture.org.uk, January 2007

Growing Schools, www.teachernet.gov.uk/growingschools, January 2007

Helen Hamlyn Research Institute, www.hhrc.rca.ac.uk, November 2006

Mobile Community Design, www.mobilecommunity.com, November 2006

O2, www.o2.org/index.php, January 2007

Platform 21 – Positive Alarm, www.platform21.com, January 2007

RED and Dott07 at The Design Council, www.designcouncil.org.uk/RED and www.dott07.com, November 2006

Royal Society of the Arts, www.rsa.org.uk, January 2007

Rural Studio, cadc.auburn.edu/soa/rural%2Dstudio/mission.htm, January 2007

SCORE, www.score-network.org/score/score_module/index.php, January 2007

Second Life, www.secondlife.com, January 2007

Slow, www.slowdesign.org, November 2006

Slow Food, www.slowfood.com, January 2007

SlowLab, www.slowlab.net, January 2007

SusProNet, www.suspronet.org, January 2007

Sustainable Everyday, www.sustainable-everyday.net, January 2007

The Green Map System, www.greenmap.com, January 2007

The Sofa Project, www.sofaproject.org.uk, January 2007

Walking Bus, www.walkingbus.com, January 2007

WBCSD, www.wbcsd.org/templates/TemplateWBCSD5/layout.asp?MenuID=1, January 2007

Wikipedia, www.wikipedia.org, January 2007

YouTube, www.youtube.com, January 2007

WHAT DOES SUSTAINABLE MEAN?

GET THE BALANCE RIGHT

overground
underground

"SUSTAINABLE DESIGN is a DESIGN APPROACH based on a philosophy of PARTICIPATION in which DESIGNERS facilitate, catalyse and enable SOCIETAL behavioural change."

DESIGNER as...
CITIZEN...
CO-DESIGNER...
SHAMAN...

PERCEPTIONS
EXPERIENCES
ARTIFACTS

OTHER ACTORS

- Yesterday's SOCIETIES PAST

- Today's SOCIETIES - the continuous PRESENT

- TOMORROW's SOCIETIES - the sustainable FUTURES

• nodes
- flows (energy, materials, ideas...)

By: Alastair Fuad-Luke

STOP ADVERTISING
CHEAP & TACKY
THROWAWAY
JUNK !!

CHERISH WHAT WE
ALREADY HAVE
KEEP IT FOREVER X

Introduction

Changes are occurring in design. We are witnessing a flourishing of diversity, complexity, playfulness, energy and freshness together with new opportunities for distributed and shared creativity. These developments are happening for a variety of reasons – economic, environmental, moral and ideological. Within an information-rich global milieu these new directions are being informed, influenced and enabled by many sources, and individual designers can make their work known to a worldwide audience. The reasons, approaches and outcomes are numerous and varied but, collectively, many of these directions indicate a burgeoning of creativity coupled with a new democratization of ideas and a heightened sense of responsibility.

However, these changes are not happening within mainstream industrial design, which seems largely out-of-touch with such developments. It may be that industrial design has been part of the corporate leviathan for so long that it is no longer able to flex its creative muscles and, unused, they have atrophied. Even where the contribution of industrial design has been most successful, in companies such as Apple and Dyson, the design contribution, while certainly accomplished, remains essentially conservative in character. In contrast, many contemporary directions outside the mainstream are indicative of a quite different sensibility. The most notable work challenges the pre-packaged homogeneity that mass-manufacturing presents as a *fait accompli* and which relegates us to passive consumers with little opportunity for deeper understanding or involvement. The new design is often more enabling, more approachable, more expressive and, consequently, more engaging. Tellingly, it can often be characterized by words prefixed by 're' – responding, restoring, recovering, remixing, recycling, re-using, reducing. It may even be about redemption. This design work may be recent, but the question it addresses is not. Implicitly, much of this work is an attempt by designers to suggest an answer to the question, 'How can we live decently?' It is the same question that Balzac asked over a century and a half ago (Gopnik, 2004) and which many others have asked before and since.

This type of design requires a process rather different from that which has been prevalent in design schools for many years. The standard 'representational' approaches, whether paper-based or computer-based, become secondary – there is greater emphasis on intuitive, hands-on, physical and reciprocal methods that respond to the world as it is. Recalling the creative flourish during the early decades of the 20th century, they involve collage, assemblage and bricolage, and, where deemed appropriate, these are used in combination with the latest technologies to provide new design possibilities. Significantly, these approaches often make use of existing objects in ways that are not only stimulating and aesthetically inspiring, but also attendant to new sensibilities and responsibilities related to social equity and the environment.

Here, I discuss several of these new directions with respect to contemporary environmental and socio-cultural concerns. However, to develop a more comprehensive appreciation of the process, and the conceptual differences between these emerging directions and products of conventional industrial design and mass-production, it is useful to actually engage in the process of designing. Therefore, several examples have been developed that explore ways of incorporating existing products in new functional designs. The process of design engagement, and reflecting on the artefacts it yields, allows for a deeper understanding of the design decisions, and the potential contributions these new directions can make to our evolving ideas of material culture.

Appreciation

The morning I sat down to write this chapter I received an email from a colleague who had just returned from a visit to India. He wrote:

> *I agree with what all great minds have said: one never comes back the same.*
> *I actually struggled with what I would say when asked 'how was India?' … I*
> *came back feeling more blessed than ever – content with what I have, and no*
> *longer desiring what I don't have (that is the most significant change) – a gift I*
> *did not expect.*
>
> *(Boulanger, 2006)*

Only the previous evening, when I had been making notes to structure this paper, I had at one point written prominently across the page, 'Appreciate – what we already have'. Implicitly, this is a significant aspect of many of the emerging directions in design, which draw upon sources that are already present within the human-made environment – the capacity that exists at the local level, as well as the unvalued detritus or forgotten products of modern society. The Sear's Style project that utilizes spare parts in new designs and the Salvation series, which uses second-hand chinaware, both by the Boyms (Boym, 2002, pp28–37, 56–61), the Multidao, Banquette and Alligator chairs of the Campana brothers, which utilize local skills and incorporate soft toys for the cushioning and upholstery (Campana and Campana, 2004), and the Kebab Lamps designed by 'Committee', made from a variety of junk stall bric-a-brac (Committee, 2006), are all examples of this design approach. They contrast starkly with conventional mass-production methods that make heavy use of virgin resources and which have such detrimental environmental and social consequences.

Being content with what we have seems to be something of a rarity in modern society. This not only seems rather sad, it is also profligate and deeply damaging. The culture of dissatisfaction that pervades the richest countries in the world is a key driver of consumerism and a critical component of our current notions of wealth creation. It is also a major contributor to environmental destruction and runs contrary to meaningful understandings of sufficiency and of human happiness (see Note 1). The imaginative directions that are emerging in contemporary design indicate that some designers are wrestling with these issues and attempting to reconcile ethical and environmental concerns within their creative endeavours. The results suggest a trajectory for design that can help reduce some of the negative consequences of consumerism and allow a re-valuing of what we already have, while also contributing to economic well-being.

Design redux

The term 'redux' was used by film director Francis Ford Coppola in 2001 when he released a newly edited version of his 1979 film, *Apocalypse Now*; in the later edition, 'Redux' was added to the title. The term, which has its origins in the 17th century, means 'bring back' or 'restore'. Coppola used it to re-present his film to a new audience, as well as to those who had seen the original version. The longer 2001 version included substantial sections of previously unseen footage, which provided a useful basis for re-marketing a significant film that was, at the time of the new release, 22 years old. Some might criticize this as a cynical way of making money from an old movie, but it can be seen as an opportunity for re-appreciating what we already have, while also generating economic activity.

The production of consumer goods, like film-making, requires ideas and efforts by many people, as well as materials and energy resources and, inevitably, a certain amount of waste, pollution and environmental damage will occur. Thus, by re-presenting and re-valuing older productions, be they films or products, we restore and re-acknowledge them as contributions to human culture. We also acknowledge the creativity, work, resources and environmental costs that have already occurred in the course of their production. In other words, we show appreciation and demonstrate respect. When income generation and aesthetic and/or technological upgrading are included, it becomes possible to create meaningful, creative work and contribute to economic interests, while simultaneously moderating both our use of materials and energy and their associated environmental effects.

Designer Jurgen Bey has taken old chairs and re-covered them in glass reinforced polyester (Ramakers and Bakker, 2004, pp32–33). In another design, he envelops an old chandelier in a cylinder of two-way mirror foil (Droog, 1999). In both these designs, older products are restored to use, made contemporary and re-appreciated. New materials are used, yes, but in relatively small quantities. In these examples, the objects have to be carefully selected. This is true too, of the Bootleg series by Wolf, Bader and Oschtz – where admired 'classic' designs of music equipment, that retain a certain design cachet, have been modified to play MP3 files (Ramakers and Bakker, 2004, p34).

The approach I take here is rather different. It is an attempt to appreciate, or re-appreciate still-functioning products that are no longer valued; those products that are so readily discarded and replaced by newer versions that are stylistically more up to date and which may have minor technical advances. These products, which are perhaps 10 to 20 years old, have no design cachet and therefore generally find their way to landfill. In addition, the focus is on electrical and electronic goods because these are especially problematic in terms of their environmental consequences (Waste Electrical and Electronic Equipment (WEEE), 2002/2003). Through discussion and designed examples, the approach illustrates a potentially constructive direction for addressing sustainable concerns within our contemporary and evolving conceptions of material culture.

Distributed and shared creativity

In developing new approaches to design, the saying, 'everyone is smarter than anyone' (Eno, 2006), is pertinent. When many people contribute, the results of our endeavours can often be significant and surprising. Today, this idea is being facilitated by the internet, where projects such as the online encyclopaedia, Wikipedia (Wikipedia, 2006), the Linux open-source operating system (Linux, 2006), and a development known as Mashup (see Note 2) are offering new kinds of solutions and new opportunities for creativity. Often these solutions can be contributed to, updated and improved by hundreds of people all over the world. For example, the web application 'YouTube' allows people to make their own video creations accessible to a worldwide audience (YouTube, 2007). The growth in these kinds of applications and their increasing influence was acknowledged recently by *Time* magazine, which named its 2006 Person of the Year 'You' (*Time*, 2006, pp12–15). In some cases, such as 'mashups', these developments utilize existing resources, which are reconstituted in new ways. While these phenomena are challenging conventional notions of authorship and intellectual property, they can also make possible a productive and creative evolution of ideas. Eno has also given the example of researchers who place their academic papers on the internet – to be aired to the scholarly community, improved upon and added to by others, as an alternative to the more usual journal publication (Eno, 2006). These recent practices have strong parallels with more ancient traditions. For example, the stories, mythologies and histories kept alive in oral cultures became compelling, intricate, relevant and profound because they were allowed to evolve over time, were contributed to by many, were changed and adapted to context and, in the process, accumulated layers of meaning and complexity. We just have to think of the many stories from the oral tradition to see that this is the case. These stories, such as the fables attributed to Aesop, the *Thousand and One Nights*, and *The Odyssey*, have stood the test of time and are still appreciated today. In a somewhat similar vein, Manzini and Jégou have developed 'Enabling Solutions', which offer a method for creating viable, affordable and desirable services at the local level, and in the process they engage people and community (Manzini and Jégou, 2003). However, in mainstream product design, practices that encourage local engagement and facilitate this kind of design evolution are far less apparent.

The example used by Thackara, of *Canto Ostinato*, is useful in indicating a way forward for design (Thackara, 2005, p211). Unlike conventional musical compositions, this piece for four pianos is far more loosely defined. The composer provides a basic structure, an idea in the form of an incomplete score. Each performance will be different because it is affected by place, audience and the players' interpretation.

When we consider these various examples in the context of design, collectively they suggest a way forward that not only challenges many of our assumptions about the role of the designer, but also offers a constructive path for incorporating sustainable concerns. Firstly, individual authorship and the customary notion that the 'designer' is the primary influence in defining the nature and appearance of products are less important here. Secondly, the contemporary norm of large companies producing virtually identical mass-produced products for wide distribution, and with little, if any, long-term responsibility for the product, is questioned. Instead, a direction is suggested that allows a continual and dynamic approach to making, adapting, recovering, restoring, re-interpreting, re-making and re-presenting; an approach that is contingent on locale, cultural preferences, local materials and skills, and local engagement. Such an approach allows the priorities of sustainability to be more easily embedded into our conceptions of material culture and thus it helps overcome a situation in which people are encouraged to be passive consumers of pre-packaged products. Material culture becomes the beneficiary of the diverse contributions of many. This not only enables us to more effectively address the serious concerns surrounding current production methods, but could also lead to a more intimate, interesting and preferred rendition of functional objects. Within such an approach, mass-production has a vital role to play. However, the dominance of mass-production, in producing complete, inviolable products for mass-consumption is challenged. Moreover, these new directions in design suggest that it may be possible to bridge the chasm that has grown between traditional craft design and industrial production, a chasm that emerged during the late 19th century when these two important approaches to production went their separate ways.

The key to progressing such directions in the field of product design seems to be the development of a way forward that enables input and engagement at the local level. As in the examples referred to above, a starting point is required that provides an idea, and a basic structure. This must be defined rather loosely, so as to enable flexible interpretation and creative engagement, at a level that is appropriate to local input. In addition, it must allow for the benefits and contribution that mass-production can offer, because it has to be recognized that not everything can be achieved locally. In terms of sustainability, in order to moderate waste and reliance on new resources, and to provide a basis for rethinking material culture, such an approach would also have to be able to address the hundreds of products that are regularly discarded. These discarded products can provide a useful starting point for considering a different path for design and provide one way of addressing Thackara's suggestion of closing the loops in the flow of materials and energy at the local level (Thackara, 2005, p226).

A design approach

In developing a way forward to address these ideas, an attempt has been made to utilize discarded, unvalued objects. Particular emphasis is placed on electronic goods as these become stylistically and/or technically outdated especially quickly and are creating a severe problem in terms of their disposal. In Canada over 272,000 tonnes of computers, phones, TVs, stereos, small appliances and other electronic waste go to landfill each year (Natural Resources Canada, 2006). However, a design approach that attempts to incorporate discarded electronic objects in new design solutions, and to do so in such a way as to include local input, faces several significant challenges.

Firstly, a standardized approach is not possible because of the sheer variety and unpredictability of these discarded 'source' materials.

Secondly, it seems propitious to develop an approach that avoids the need for product disassembly. To break down the products into their component parts would be time consuming and expensive, and would inevitably create waste. It would also require sophisticated and expensive technical expertise in order to find new uses for these components. An alternative is to use the products as they are and, through design, offer opportunities for them to be re-valued. This is also in accord with the first two, and more important, of the three R's – Reduce and Re-use; only after these options are attempted should we consider Recycling.

Thirdly, local engagement and input would be facilitated by devising an approach that requires little in the way of capital investment, but rather makes use of relatively low-tech and/or inexpensive methods to achieve new design solutions.

Lastly, the design challenge here is not to prescribe a stepwise method, nor to develop a finished product (except for purposes of illustration) but to provide enough of a structure or idea that will allow people at the local level to create finished designs that are contingent, infinitely variable, dependent on context, attendant to notions of reduction, moderation and appreciation, and which can ameliorate, in many small ways, the problems associated with disposal and waste. Such a direction would not only enable new renditions of functional objects to be developed and environmental issues to be addressed, it could also serve the community by providing locally available, creative work and local opportunities for product re-use, re-production, repair and recovery.

These considerations are consistent with Thackara's seven design frameworks of, *sense and respond; deep context; seeding edge effects; smart recombination; social fiction; designing with us;* and *design as service* (Thackara, 2005, p213). The phenomenon of 'remix' in contemporary music, which is also an aspect of Mashup (see above), has somewhat similar characteristics to this type of design approach, where segments of pre-existing music or speech are put together in creative combinations to create new musical works. Older, perhaps forgotten, songs and videos are fused together into a new whole and, through this process, they can be appreciated by a new audience. An example of Mashup in music is a recent production of The Beatles' music for the Canada-based circus theatre company Cirque du Soleil. Here, the original music is put together in new combinations, 'mashed up', added to with new composition, speeded up, slowed down and reversed (Martin and Martin, 2006). The result is a fresh, contemporary rendition of very familiar music. Similar developments are affecting other areas of human creativity. Scripts of old plays are being manipulated and edited, and new material is being added to create radically new creations that are relevant to a contemporary audience. For example, a play at the Hampstead Theatre in London, entitled *Faustus*, combines parts of Christopher Marlowe's Doctor Faustus, written in the 16th century, with material from the 2003 'Insult to Injury' project by British artists, the Chapman brothers (Haydon, 2006).

In such approaches, the already existing, human-made environment is 'mined' for resources, which then form the material for new creations. This constant borrowing, appropriation and re-use, across many fields, is a growing characteristic of our time. It challenges our conventions, because there is often less concern with traditional boundaries and established notions of attribution. In previous times, the resources of the natural world were 'harvested' at will, without too much regard for consequences, but today, such methods are becoming increasingly difficult to justify. It therefore seems appropriate, and more consistent with sustainable principles, to consider the discarded and forgotten products of modern society, and to draw on these as a basis for creating new design opportunities.

Process

To address the challenges posed by 'the local' it is necessary to adopt a design process that is flexible and responsive to the diversity that exists at the small, particular, local level and within those areas that are immediate, physical and cognitive. Planning ahead, with fixed ideas, becomes an obstacle. It is important to allow a more intuitive process that attempts to relate a plethora of complex, interdependent 'background' ideas and understandings about products, the environment, people and function. The result of this way of working is, in any single design example, imperfect and partial – to which we can respond again, using it as a basis for reflection, and move to the next attempt, which will be informed by new ideas suggested by the previous piece, together with other ideas from readings, observations and further reflection. Whether or not such a process is considered valid depends on what we are attempting to achieve and the criteria we use to validate. However, it is an approach that is modest and deeply grounded in an interdependent relationship between the rational and the intuitive, the functional and the aesthetic; far more so, in my view, than the large-scale, rationalized approaches to product design and production that tend to dominate our culture. This smaller, more local, and more direct approach draws upon tacit knowledge, responds directly to local conditions, can yield solutions that address sustainable concerns, and can contribute to the development of a more varied and potentially more desirable rendition of functional objects.

Harvesting the discarded

The intention in this design exercise was to explore ways of re-using discarded products that could be found locally. In addition, it was necessary to effect such re-use in a manner that was suited to small scale, and which would provide a feasible basis or template for adoption and adaptation by others, in other regions. For the reasons outlined earlier, emphasis was placed on the re-use of objects with little or no modification, rather than on disassembly. Consideration was given to the nature and form of local input, as well as to the incorporation of new components or products that would enable the discarded products to have a new life in an acceptable manner. In summary, a design approach was required that:

- would make use of readily available, old, unwanted products;
- can be achieved locally;
- is highly flexible in its ability to incorporate a wide variety of products or product combinations;
- enables people at the local level to develop design variations that appeal to their own tastes and reflect aesthetic or cultural preferences;
- retrieves, re-uses, re-appreciates and re-presents objects in ways that are useful and desirable:
- contributes to the reduction of waste and helps moderate the requirement and desire for 'new' objects.

An enabling proposition

A feasible way forward depends on the development of an idea, or basic structure, that enables new design solutions to be developed. The following examples are all based on a simple 'frame' that provides the foundation for a new functional composition. The use of the frame stems from earlier work that looked at issues such as product form (Walker, 2006, pp139–166) and ephemerality. Here, it is used again but for different reasons. It serves a number of purposes that collectively allow old, rejected objects to be seen and valued anew.

Chapman has suggested that for people to maintain a prolonged engagement with functional products, designers should explore ways forward that support continued growth and evolution; to re-fashion the interaction in order to facilitate an ongoing relationship (Chapman, 2005, p186). The 'frame' proposed here is one example of how this might be achieved. Essentially, it serves as an enabling device that allows the user to see the object as an element within a newly defined, discrete and particular context. The frame separates the object from its surroundings and places it within a specially designed composition. In doing so, the discarded object becomes one element within this new composition and, in the process, it becomes re-contextualized. It is an essential compositional constituent that contributes materially to a new, functional whole. In addition, the intrinsic qualities of the object, that is, its outdated aesthetic qualities – its form, its colours and its worn or damaged surfaces – become essential qualitative characteristics of this new whole.

Figure 3.1 WineLight: re-used bottles, new electrical fittings, shades and low-energy bulbs mounted on a locally made white frame with shelf (MDF and pine)

Within this separated frame, individual elements and the entire composition

Figure 3.2 RePlay: re-used 1980s cassette player, new MP3 player, mounted on a locally made white frame with shelf (MDF and pine)

Figure 3.3 ReCast: re-used 1970s radio, new iPod, mounted on a locally made frame (MDF and pine) with vintage wallpaper and shelf finished in wood-grain adhesive plastic film

can diverge considerably from our usual ideas of what is appealing and tasteful – and yet can still be regarded as having aesthetic appeal. The intentional separation from the surroundings, through the use of the frame, suggests that this can indeed be the case. Thus, the use of the frame appears effectively to enable a wide variety of objects to be used again. At this point, it is relevant to note that mass-produced consumer products are designed to be used within a broad range of domestic contexts. However, as particular products age, they become increasingly undesirable, often because they are regarded as no longer appropriate or pleasing within their specific context of use. Products are associated with social standing and personal expression and so, as objects become old and shabby, they are replaced. The re-presentation of objects within a specifically defined context offers one example of how older, perhaps deteriorated products, can be re-appreciated. The frame serves a similar purpose to the rarefied context of the white cube art gallery. Both have the effect of elevating the objects or art pieces. While some artists regard this as inappropriate and challenge it in their work (Veiteburg, 2004), perhaps it is exactly what is needed in the case of lowly and otherwise discarded consumer products because it allows them to be re-noticed, re-used and re-valued.

Thus, the frame is a way of addressing, through design, a sustained engagement with objects. It offers one approach to building more sustainable narratives and an alternative to the 'box fresh' ideal of newness so prevalent in contemporary culture (Chapman, 2005, pp111, 132).

As a locally achievable, sustainable solution, the frame:

- can be built in a simple workshop using a variety of readily available materials such as softwoods and sheet stock (medium density fibreboard (MDF), plywood, etc.);
- has variable dimensions, which can be specified to suit a wide diversity of locally available discarded objects and other compositional elements;
- provides a foundation for the application of many different finishes to suit local preferences, as well as finishes tailored to be compatible with the compositional components;
- provides an easily changeable foundation for the composition itself, and allows for the integration of locally available mass-produced and locally produced elements, as well as the combination of new elements with old;
- facilitates reduction, re-use, and recovery through aesthetically varied, locally created and potentially desirable design solutions;
- offers a means for re-using products in a potentially cost effective, locally appropriate manner;
- offers a means for developing local employment that could reduce electronic waste while providing creative work opportunities.

Thus, the frame concept appears to be an effective, locally enabling device that provides a basis for exploring sustainable product solutions. It is not prescriptive, but provides a highly flexible basis for local interpretation and for a wide variety of design solutions.

A number of examples have been created to illustrate the idea. WineLight (Figure 3.1) is a wall sconce comprising three re-used wine bottles combined with new, off-the-shelf electrical parts and mounted on a white frame with shelf, constructed from pine and MDF. RePlay (Figure 3.2) combines a 1980s vintage cassette/radio with a new MP3 player, again mounted on a locally produced white frame with shelf. ReCast (Figure 3.3) uses a 1970s

vintage radio as the speaker output for an iPod; in this case the frame was finished in a patterned wallpaper and other elements added to complete the functional composition. This example also explores notions of taste and, compared to the earlier examples, illustrates that the basic frame device allows for a variety of aesthetic possibilities. ReCall (Figure 3.4), a re-presentation of a 1980s wall phone, uses the 'canvas' of the frame as a basis for re-contextualizing the 'discarded' object – in this case with a painted background and the addition of elements suggestive of a somewhat institutional, rather than domestic, context.

Figure 3.4 ReCall: re-used 1980s telephone, mounted on a locally made frame (MDF and pine) with latex paint finish, doodles, notes and pencil on cord.

Re-valuing objects

Walker and Chaplin (1997, pp165–166) have distinguished several kinds of value that can be attributed to an artefact:

- *Artistic* value – intrinsic excellence, aesthetic quality, significant content.
- *Use* value – practical function irrespective of appearance and aesthetic attributes. (This can also include decorative, symbolic, memorial, ideological and political value.)
- *Sentimental* value – private, biographical and emotional life of an individual.
- *Exchange* value – monetary value is variable because of fluctuations in the market and the economy.

In several of the re-used artefacts presented here, the original value would have been primarily their use value, coupled with their 'newness' – that is, aesthetic attributes related to the perception of innovation or fashion. Thus, their exchange value within the then current market was dependent, to a significant degree, on their perceived newness in functionality and aesthetics. Over time, both functionality and aesthetic attributes become outdated, relative to later models, and so the value of those attributes becomes diminished, which is reflected in the minimal exchange value of such objects.

In re-presenting the artefacts within functional compositions, as illustrated, artistic or aesthetic value can be restored – partly by presenting the artefacts as components within larger, aesthetically sensitive assemblages, and partly because within these compositions their old-fashioned styling can be appreciated (i.e. valued) anew. This is because the reappearance of a rejected or discarded object within a contemporary composition can afford the object a fresh decorative value. Moreover, if the underlying basis of such a re-presentation is understood as a contribution to design for sustainability, the composition can also acquire a certain ideological or even political value. In addition, the fact that the re-presented product is old-fashioned can mean that, within the functional composition, it acquires a certain sentimental value – stimulating memories of an earlier time. Lastly, when the old product is combined with new technology to provide a new functionality, its use value becomes reinstated.

Thus, the functional composition or 'design redux', as presented here, would seem to be one avenue for designers fruitfully to explore in their attempts to address sustainable concerns. It offers a means for restoring value to rejected objects in a manner that touches upon all the categories of artefact value identified by Walker and Chaplin. In the process, it contributes to a re-appreciation of existing artefacts, and can help moderate the need for new artefacts, and help reduce the number of older products entering landfill.

Notes

1   Spiritual teaching from around the world, from the Bhagavad Gita to the Gospels, has taught that material possessions can be impediments to happiness and contentment. Many contemporary studies tend to be in accord with these teachings. Although results of research into 'happiness' differ, as would be expected with such a subjective notion, a 2003 study published in *New Scientist* suggested that wealth is not directly linked to happiness and that many of the world's happiest people live in poorer countries. Key criteria for happiness included a genetic propensity to happiness, marriage, friends and desiring less (BBC, 2003). In a 2006 UK study, researchers suggested that consumerism is related to unchanging 'happiness' trends (Easton, 2006). The conclusions of a recent study, again published in *New Scientist*, have bucked this trend to some extent, suggesting that those living in the wealthiest countries are among the happiest. However, even here, the main criteria for happiness tend to be associated with health and

education, with economic security also being a factor (Khamsi, 2006). A survey on 'happiness' in British Columbia in August 2006 identified the key 'happiness' factors as family, friends, career/work, health and personal freedom (Mustel, 2006).

2   'Mashup' is a term that applies to utilizing digital data from different sources and recombining them in new ways. The term refers to the phenomenon of remixing in music and video as well as other web-based applications. Google maps, for example, have been combined with information from other sources to produce useful solutions for particular interest groups. A general introduction to Mashup is available at Wikipedia at: http://en.wikipedia.org/wiki/Mashup (web_application_hybrid), accessed 28 December 2006.

An article describing Google maps mashups is available at: www.javaworld.com/javaworld/jw-01-2006/jw-0116-google.html, accessed 28 December 2006.

An earlier version of this chapter was presented at the European Academy of Design Conference, Izmir, Turkey, April 2007.

References

BBC (2003) 'Nigeria tops happiness survey', BBC NEWS, 2 October, http://news.bbc.co.uk/go/pr/fr/-/2/hi/africa/3157570.stm, accessed 30 October 2006

Boulanger, S. Personal correspondence, 30 October 2006, Director of Design, BoldWing Continuum Architects Inc., with permission

Boym, C. (2002) *Curious Boym*, Princeton Architectural Press, New York

Campana, F. and Campana, H. (2004) 'Zest for Life', Design Museum, London

Chapman, J. (2005) *Emotionally Durable Design: Objects, Experiences and Empathy*, Earthscan, London

Committee (2006) 'Design Mart', Design Museum Exhibition, London, 14 January to 19 February, www.designmuseum.org/design/committee, accessed 27 January 2007

Droog (1999) www.droogdesign.nl, accessed 28 December 2006

Easton, M. (2006) 'Britain's happiness in decline', BBC News, 3 May, 2006, http://news.bbc.co.uk/go/pr/fr/-/1/hi/programmes/happiness_formula/4771908.stm, accessed 30 October

Eno, B. (2006) 'Free thinking festival', opening lecture, broadcast on BBC Radio 3, Friday 3 November, www.bbc.co.uk/radio3/freethinking2006/pip/132yy/, accessed 3 November 2006

Gopnik, A. (2004) Introduction to *The Wrong Side of Paris* by Honoré De Balzac, Random House, New York

Haydon, A. (2006) Review of *Faustus*, Hampstead Theatre, London, 26 October, www.culturewars.org.uk/2006-01/faustus.htm, accessed 19 November 2006

Khamsi, R. (2006) 'Wealthy nations hold the keys to happiness', NewScientist.com news service, 28 July, www.newscientist.com/channel/being-human/dn9642-wealthy-nations-hold-the-keys-to-happiness.html, accessed 30 October 2006

Linux (2006) www.linux.org, accessed 28 December 2006

Manzini, E. and Jégou, F. (2003) *Sustainable Everyday: Scenarios of Urban Life*, Edizioni Ambiente, Milan

Martin, G. and Martin, G. (2006) 'The Beatles "Love"', liner notes to CD, EMI Music Canada, Mississauga, Ontario

Mustel (2006) *August 2006 Happiness Survey*, for British Columbia, Canada, The Mustel Group, Market Research, www.mustelgroup.com/pdf/a498hs_jha.pdf, accessed 30 October 2006

Natural Resources Canada (2006) 'Electronics waste: Making mountains out of megabytes', *Natural Elements*, www.nrcan.gc.ca/elements/issues/06/e-recycle_e.html, accessed 18 July 2006

Ramakers, R. and Bakker, G. (2004) *Simply Droog*, Droog, Amsterdam

Thackara, J. (2005) *In the Bubble: Designing in a Complex World*, The MIT Press, Cambridge, Massachusetts

Time (2006) 'Time Person of the Year – You', Canadian Edition, 25 December 2006 / 1 January 2007

Veiteberg, J. (2004) 'Hybrid practice: A craft intervention in a contemporary art arena', Challenging Craft Conference, Greys School of Art, Aberdeen, 8–10 September, www2.rgu.ac.uk/challengingcraft/ChallengingCraft/papers/jorunnveiteberg/jveitebergabstract.htm, accessed 6 May 2007

Walker J. A. and Chaplin, S. (1997) *Visual Culture: An Introduction*, Manchester University Press, Manchester

Walker, S. (2006) *Sustainable by Design: Explorations in Theory and Practice*, Earthscan, London

WEEE (Waste Electrical and Electronic Equipment) Directives 2002/96/EC and 2003/108/EC, www.netregs.gov.uk/netregs/275207/1631119/?version=1&lang=_e, accessed 28 December 2006

Wikipedia (2006) http://en.wikipedia.org/wiki/Main_Page, accessed 28 December 2006

YouTube (2007) www.youtube.com, accessed 24 January 2007

Chapter 4

Ezio Manzini
The Scenario of a Multi-local Society:
Creative Communities, Active Networks
and Enabling Solutions

In these difficult times, optimism is an ethical duty.

Considering the present conditions of our planet and the catastrophic nature of current major trends, we should ask ourselves what the effective role of design has been up to now. Unfortunately, the answer is only too clear. Generally speaking, design has been, and still is, 'part of the problem'.

However, this is not an inevitable destiny. Design can and must play another role and become instead 'part of the solution'. It can do so because within its 'genetic code' there is the idea that its raison d'être is to improve the quality of the world. And it is from here that we have to start again, reassessing the quality of the world that design, following its deep ethical mission, should improve.

Given that, we can assume that design can actually be part of the solution because it is the social actor that above all others, by its very nature, has to do with the everyday relationships of human beings with their artefacts. It is precisely these relationships, together with the expectations of well-being that are built on them, that must change in the near future, during the transition towards sustainability. So, on these grounds, design has its own responsibilities. But it also holds a very special kind of power: a power that is at the same time both very weak and very strong. It is very weak because it has no means of imposing its view on others, but very strong because it does have the tools to operate on the quality of things, and their acceptability, and therefore on the attraction of the scenarios of well-being they help to generate. Its specific characteristic in the great social learning process that awaits us is therefore to offer new solutions to problems, both old and new, and to place scenarios onto the social discussion table, collaborating in the building of shared visions on possible, sustainable futures.

In the following notes I will propose some steps in this direction. And specifically, in the direction of building a new scenario, which will be called the 'scenario of the multi-local society'.

Before doing that, it has to be said, and underlined, that the scenario building exercise that I am going to propose, as with every scenario building process, is not a 'neutral' or a 'scientific' activity. This activity is always, and this time more than usual, the result of design choices: from the complexity of society, from the contradictory signals that it emits, the scenario building process consists of extracting those tendencies and those weak signals that, put together and correctly interpreted, can generate a new and motivated vision of the present and of its possible evolution in order to give a reference to our daily concrete actions.

In other words, to (collaborate to) build possible scenarios of sustainable society is the first and fundamental step to shift the designers' role from the side of the problem generators to the one of the solution promoters.

In the following chapters this scenario building exercise will be carried out introducing some *promising cases* of social innovation (the *creative communities* and the *collaborative networks*) and discussing the possibility/opportunity of moving from them to outline a new and practicable vision of a sustainable future: the *multi-local society*. A vision that should have the capability to catalyse the action of different social actors in a sustainable direction.

Promising cases: Creative communities and collaborative networks

Transition towards sustainability requires radical changes in the way we produce and consume and, in general, in the way we live. In fact, we need to learn how to *live better* (the entire population of the planet) and, at the same time, *reduce our ecological footprint* and *improve the quality of our social fabric*. The link between the environmental and social dimensions of this problem clearly appears in this framework, showing that *radical social innovation*[1] will be needed, in order to move from current unsustainable models to new sustainable ones.

Given the nature and the dimension of this change, we have to see transition towards sustainability (and, in particular, towards sustainable ways of living) as a *wide-reaching social learning process* in which the most diversified forms of knowledge and organizational capabilities must be valorized in the most *open* and *flexible* way. Among these, a particular role will be played by local initiatives that, in some ways, can be seen as signals of new behaviours and new ways of thinking.

How do we recognize these signals of social innovation? How do we recognize where 'the new' comes from? And how do we recognize if and when it can be considered as a step in the direction of sustainability? In order to answer these questions our starting point is the observation that, in the framework of the contemporary society, cases of social innovation are continuously emerging in the form of new behaviours, new forms of organization, new ways of living. Some of them are even more unsustainable than the previous ones, but some others appear as interesting moves towards more sustainable ways of living. These cases may be defined as *promising cases*; that is, examples of initiatives where, in different ways and for different motivations, some people have re-oriented their behaviours and their expectations in a direction that appears to be coherent with the principles of social and environmental sustainability.

Even if, at the moment, these promising cases are the expression of social minorities, and confronted with mainstream ways of thinking and behaving many of them tend to disappear, they are crucial for promoting and orienting the transition towards sustainability. In fact they present themselves as social experiments and, as a whole, as a *large laboratory of possible futures*. A laboratory where different ways of moving towards sustainability may be searched and assessed. As in every laboratory, nobody can *a priori* say which experiment will be really successful. Nevertheless, every attempt may give some useful experiences if we are able to recognize them and to learn from them.

In the following notes I will consider two clusters of promising cases: *creative communities* and *collaborative networks*.

Creative communities

Observing society as a whole and in all its contradictoriness, we can see that, alongside numerous worrying tendencies, signals are also emerging that indicate different and far more promising developments. Signals, still weak, but all the same stating clearly that another way of being and doing is possible. As examples, groups of people or communities that act together to:

- reorganize the way they live in their homes (as in the *co-housing* movement) and their neighbourhood (bringing it to life; creating the conditions for children to go to school on foot; fostering mobility on foot or by bike);
- develop new participatory social services for the elderly and for parents (such as the young and the elderly living together or micro-nurseries set up and managed by enterprising mothers);
- set up food networks fostering producers of organic items, and promoting the quality and typical characteristics of their products (as with the Slow Food movement, solidarity purchasing groups and fair trade organizations).[2]

The list of examples could continue showing their variety, but also their common denominators.[3]

In fact, considered as a whole, these promising cases tell us that, already today, it is possible to do things differently and consider one's own work, one's own time and one's own system of social relationships in a different light. They show that there are people who are able to act outside the dominant thought and behaviour pattern and organize themselves, and cooperate with others, to achieve concrete, positive results.

We will refer to them as *creative communities*: groups of innovative citizens organizing themselves to solve a problem or to open a new possibility, and doing so as a positive step in the social learning process towards social and environmental sustainability.[4]

Collaborative networks

Something very interesting is happening in the field of organization and in the ways in which people participate in collaborative projects. The starting point of this phenomenon is the organizational model emerging from the Open Source software movement.[5]

Over the last decade the principles behind this highly collaborative approach have increasingly been applied to areas beyond the coding of software (Lessig, 2001; Stalder and Hirsh, 2002). And now, we can observe that these principles have been highly successful in proposing collaborative and effective organizational models in several other application fields. Examples include:

- the building of new common knowledge, as in the case of *Wikipedia*, the encyclopaedia that, in few years, has become the largest in the world;
- the realization of new forms of social organization, like *Meet-Up, SmartMobs* and the BBC's *Action Network*, which links people interested in doing something collectively (from renting a bus for a journey, to cleaning a river bank) and, once the necessary critical mass is achieved, supports them in doing it;
- the application of the peer-to-peer approach to health care activities, as in the case of *Open Welfare*, a project led by the British Design Council.

The innovative character of these new models has to be underlined. All these examples of *collaborative networks* are characterized by motivations and methods that were unimaginable a few years ago, but are now the norm. Large numbers of interested people may be brought together and organized to build a common vision and a common direction, and to develop even very complex projects on a global scale (as in Wikipedia) or locally (as in Meet-Up, SmartMobs and Action Network). Quoting the British Design Council, which refers to them as *open models*, they are new forms of organization that do not rely 'on mass participation in the creation of the service. The boundary is blurred between the users and producers of a service. It is effectively often impossible to differentiate between those who are creating the service and those who are the consumers or users of the output' (Cottam and Leadbeater, 2004b).

A possible convergence

To conclude this part, it is useful to underline that *creative communities* and *collaborative networks*, until now, have been two different and rather separate phenomena. Except for some minor overlapping, they have been generated by different people with different motivations. Nevertheless, I think that, in the near future, they will converge and become a unique complex dynamic of social change. Doing so, they will strongly reinforce each other: creative communities will bring the lively richness of people involved in real, daily problems, and collaborative networks the new opportunities that have been opened by their brand new forms of organization.[6]

But there is another important reason why they and their possible convergence are so significant. Together, they can become the building blocks of a new vision: the vision of sustainable *multi-local society*. A society based on a new relation between 'local' and 'global'.

Vision: Multi-local society and distributed economies

Contrary to what was thought in the past, the joint phenomena of globalization and increased connectivity have given rise once again to the local dimension. By the expression 'local', what is meant now is something very removed from what was understood in the past (i.e. the valley, the village, the small provincial town, all isolated and relatively closed within their own cultures and economies). The new local combines the specific features of places and their communities with the new phenomena generated and supported worldwide by globalization and by cultural, socio-economic interconnection.

As a matter of fact what we see are *creative communities* and *cooperative networks* which invent unprecedented cultural activities, forms of organization and economic models that are the point of intersection of two complementary strategies: a balanced interaction between the local and the global dimensions, on the one hand, and a sustainable enhancement of local (physical and socio-cultural) resources, on the other.

What appears is a kind of *cosmopolitan localism* (Sachs, 1998; Manzini and Vugliano, 2000; Manzini and Jégou, 2003), the result of a particular condition characterized by the balance between being localized (rooted in a place and in the community related to that place) and open to global flows of ideas, information, people, things and money (Appandurai, 1990). This is quite a delicate balance as, at any time, one side can prevail over the other, leading to an anti-historical closure or, alternatively, it can lead to a destructive openness of the local social fabric and its peculiar features.

Creative communities, cooperative networks and *cosmopolitan localism* are, as it has been said, the building blocks for a new vision: the vision of a sustainable society that can be defined as a *multi-local society*. That is, a network of interconnected communities and places, at the same time open and localized.

Small is not small and local is not local

In the framework of the multi-local society the dominant ideas of 'global' and 'local', and 'large' and 'small' are challenged. In fact, the multi-local society is, in nature, a highly connected world. And, in this kind of world, *the small is not small*: it is, or can be, instead a knot in a network (the real dimension of which is given by the number of links with other elements of the system). Similarly, and for the same reasons, *the local is not local*, but it is, or can be, a locally based, cosmopolitan community.

In this conceptual and practical framework, the *multi-local society* appears as a society based on communities and places[7] that are, at the same time, strong in their own identity, embedded in a physical place *and* open and connected to other places/communities.[8]

In other words: in the multi-local society, communities and places are junctions of a network, points of connection among short networks, which generate and regenerate the local social and production fabric and long networks, which connect that place and that community with the rest of the world (De Rita and Bonomi, 1998). Junctions connect 'long global networks' with 'short local networks' and, in doing so, provide support to organizational forms and production and service systems based on the *subsidiary principle* (i.e. to do on a larger scale only what cannot be done on a smaller scale, at a local level).

Today, the vision of the multi-local society is still far from mainstream, but it indicates a direction that, for several reasons, can be successfully undertaken. In fact, not only is it *locally practicable*, given that, as has been said, it is based on *real cases of social innovation* (the creative communities and the collaborative networks), but it is also coherent with another *strong driver of change*: the rise of the *distributed economies* as a potentially successful option.

Distributed economies as a viable option

In recent years the adjective *'distributed'* has been increasingly used in relation to several different socio-economic systems: information technologies, and *distributed computing*; energy systems and *distributed generation*; production and the possibilities of *distributed manufacturing*; the processes of change and *distributed innovation, distributed creativity, distributed knowledge*. And, finally, in relation to the overall socio-technical systems, the rise of new, more effective economic models: the *distributed economies*.

Some of these concepts became mainstream two decades ago (the 'classic' being distributed computing). Some of them have a strong position in the international arena (as the concepts of distributed generation and distributed manufacturing). Some have emerged in recent years, others are currently developing and they have a wide and growing audience (distributed innovation, distributed creativity, distributed intelligence and distributed economy).

In all these cases, what the term *distributed*[9] adds to the substantive to which it is related, is the idea that it has to be considered as a web of *interconnected, autonomous elements*, that is, elements that are capable of operating autonomously, and being, at the same time, highly connected with the other elements of the system.

In different words, what the adjective 'distributed' indicated is the existence of a *horizontal system architecture* in which complex activities are accomplished in parallel by a high number of connected elements (technological artefacts and/or human beings).

Considered as a whole, the diffusion of this particular system architecture can be seen as the result of two major *drivers* and a new *technological platform*, defined as follows:

- *techno-economic driver*: the search for flexibility, effectiveness, waste reduction, system robustness and security;
- *socio-cultural driver*: the search for being creative, autonomous and responsible, as a basic human inclination, particularly developed in the contemporary society among a growing group of people;
- *new technological platform*: the present higher degree of connectivity and the possibility that it offers to manage very complex systems.

The perspective of the distributed systems could be an interesting model per se: a very productive line of socio-technical innovation to be explored in all its possibilities. But the same perspective becomes even more important when its environmental, social, cultural and political implications are considered:

- *Socio-economic implications*: distributed economies make up a large part of the value creation process at the local level, generating and maintaining local wealth and local jobs. At the same time as intensifying local activities and interactions, they reinforce the *social fabric* and prepare a favourable ground to optimize the use of, and to regenerate, the existing *social resources*.
- *Environmental implications*: reducing the scale of their individual elements, distributed systems enable optimum use of local resources and facilitate forms of industrial symbiosis (thereby, reducing waste). In parallel to that, bringing the production nearer to both local resources and final users reduces transport requirements and, therefore, congestion and pollution.
- *Political implications*: bringing the power of decision nearer to the final users and increasing the visibility of the systems on which decisions have to be taken, the distributed systems facilitate democratic discussions and choices. In particular, given that the advantages and problems related to a choice can be better compared, they facilitate individuals and communities taking responsible decisions.

Whether it is possible to develop distribution systems with positive environmental, socio-economic and political implications depends on several things. Of particular importance is better understanding of the systems' potentials, and the ability to identify situations in which a system could be successfully utilized.

Local productions for multi-local markets

An early success story of the distributed economies is related to the *rediscovery of the 'local'*, in the framework of the cosmopolitan localism that we introduced at the beginning of this chapter. In this perspective, *successful local products emerge, which are linked to the place of origin and to the cultural and social values that characterize their conception and production.* The most commonly known and quoted examples are quality wine and some niche food products, such as those promoted by Slow Food. But also non-food products can be quoted; for example, the essential oils of the Provence region, the Murano glassware and the Casentino wool – all products that convey the spirit and history of a place and a community to the end consumer.[10]

The success of some local products on the global markets is the most visible part of the rediscovery of the 'local'. But there is also another, less visible, but even more important side of the story: that of *local products for local markets* – direct links being established between local producers and the consumer communities. This possibility is particularly clear in the case of food, where innovative, localized, de-intermediated *food networks* are appearing (for example, purchasing groups, community based agriculture, farmers' markets and vegetable subscriptions). But something similar can be found for some other local traditional products and for the *local use of renewable energy* (a particularly important point, which will be dealt with in the next paragraph).[11]

Distributed intelligence and distributed energy

Another, even more important, success story in the perspective of the distributed economies is the one of the *distributed intelligence*. In fact, it is well known and recognized that the internet and the increasing computing potentialities have generated, and are still generating, a new form of distributed intelligence of the socio-technical systems.

The implications of this phenomenon are radical changes in the organization of the socio-technical system: the solid and vertical organizations that have been considered – and still are – dominant in the industrialized society, are melting into fluid and horizontal ones. New distributed forms of knowledge and decision making are appearing. The dimension and the power of this phenomenon are today commonly recognized. What is not totally understood are its potentialities and implications. We can say, for instance, that all the other phenomena of socio-technical innovation that we are dealing with in this text have to be seen as direct or indirect implications of this first one.

This is the case, for instance, of the *distributed power generation*. This expression usually refers to an energy system (mainly) based on *interconnected small and medium-size power generators and/or renewable energy plants*. It implies a radical change in the dominant idea of electrical systems. But not only that – there is the possibility of a new relationship between communities and their technological assets and, perhaps, a more democratic way of managing the energy system.

Today, even if it is not yet the mainstream strategy, the option of distributed generation is largely recognized as a very promising one and its implementation has been enhanced in several different contexts, both in dense urban areas and the countryside, and in the north and south of the world. The distributed power option has been made possible thanks to the convergence of several factors, such as the existence of highly effective small and medium-size power generators and the possibility of basing the new energy systems on an intelligent information network.

The integration of distributed intelligence and distributed generation can be seen as the pillar of a new infrastructure: the *distributed infrastructure of a multi-local society.*

Actions: Enabling solutions and a new idea of industrialization

For business and institutions, the promising cases and the distributed economies perspectives point to interesting lines of research and express the demand for new generation products and services that could make these initiatives more accessible and more effective – environmentally, socially and economically.

Let us take as examples the cases of the creative communities we mentioned before. Creative communities are such because, in their own context, they have invented different ways of behaving and thinking. Looking at them more closely we realize that they emerge in very specific conditions and, above all, they are the result of the enterprise of very special people – those who have been able to think and act by breaking out of the cage of dominant thought and behaviour. Although this almost heroic aspect is the most fascinating side of these phenomena, it is also an objective limit to their diffusion (and often also of their lasting power): exceptional people are not so common and, above all, they are not immortal.

To help these ways of doing things persist and spread we must therefore start with these experiences, and the organizational model they have invented and brought to life, and propose products and services specifically conceived to increase their accessibility. In other words we have to imagine and enact *enabling solutions,* that is, systems that provide cognitive, technical and organizational instruments that enable individuals and/or communities to achieve a result, using their skills and abilities to the best advantage and, at the same time, improve their quality of life.[12]

For example, a parents' group could be assisted in starting up a micro-nursery by an enabling solution that includes, not only a step by step procedure, but also a system of guarantees that certify the suitability of the parent-organizer and the premises, and health and educational support for problems that cannot be solved within the nursery itself. Similarly, a solidarity purchasing group could be supported by special software designed to manage shopping and guarantee relationships with producers; a co-housing project could be facilitated by a system that puts potential participants in touch, helps find suitable buildings or building plots, and helps overcome any administrative and financial difficulties … the list of examples could continue.

What these examples tell us is that, case by case, enabling solutions can be thought up which, starting from what the organizers are able to do, can supply support at the weak points, integrating such knowledge and abilities that prove to be missing. The concept of enabling solution therefore indicates a line of research concerning the possibility of developing systems of products, services and knowledge conceived as systems that increase and strengthen individual and collective opportunities. Systems that make given results accessible by actively involving users in bringing them about. In carrying out this role, a special type of solution intelligence has to be brought into play: an intelligence that has to be capable of stimulating, developing and regenerating the ability and competence of those who use it.[13]

The same cases of social innovation can also express a demand that goes beyond the existing technologies and that indicates new, *socially driven lines of research*. For instance, experience of shared living facilities could become the starting point for a new generation of apparatus for totally new domestic and residential functions. Solutions that make a healthier diet and direct relations with producers possible could be stimuli for a new rationale in nutrition lines. Cases of localized production and self-production could spur the development of processes and products specifically conceived for this kind of decentralized production. Experience of mobility systems alternative to the car monoculture could lead to the development of alternative means of transport. And so on.

When addressing these issues, and the nature of the services they require, it becomes apparent that in most cases these are *complex and contextualized services*. And that they require the collaboration of various players: private firms, public institutions, voluntary associations and, directly or indirectly, the end users themselves. These characteristics mean we can refer to them as *partner-based solutions* – solutions that require the involvement of several partners.[14]

System organizers and solution providers

To respond to the previous demands, and to develop and deliver partner-based solutions, companies have to change, and adopt a role of *systems organizers* and *solution providers*. That means that they have to know how to organize systems of products and services designed for joint use and suited to the customer's specific needs and context.

Even if companies themselves, in principle, agree on the necessity and the opportunity to move in this direction, the shift towards becoming a system organizer and solution provider is not easy. In fact, it means that a company must relate to clients, other companies (often even competitors) and other stakeholders in a completely new way. It means looking at clients and groups of clients (e.g. the 'creative communities') in their specific environment and considering other companies and stakeholders as partners in the process of generating, providing and delivering solutions.

Finally, it has to be underlined that, from the companies' point of view, what has to be considered is not only the issue of how to promote 'sustainable solutions', but also that of conceiving and developing *'industrialized, sustainable solutions'*. And, in developing industrialized, sustainable solutions, problems and difficulties that may arise are related not only to the complexity of the results that we want to achieve (the *solutions*) and to the difficulty of conceiving them as sustainable systems (the *sustainable solutions*), but also to the way in which the product-service systems that enable these sustainable results may be 'systemized' to become the outputs of a real industrial activity (the *industrialized sustainable solutions*).

A new idea of industrialization

The concept of industrialized sustainable solution has to be better defined. To adopt it means to move from the traditional idea of *product-oriented linear production* to a new idea of *service-oriented networked production* – a production where the main results are services and where the production system is a socio-technical system built by a variety of actors.

This change leads to a new idea of industrialization in which the best of the *local* and *global* knowledge is used to generate a highly effective and efficient socio-technical system, and in which a *variable* set of *various* actors and entities has to be made more effective and efficient. An industrialization where the search for effectiveness and efficiency has more to do with the *economy of scope* than the economy of scale, and more with a *bottom-up approach* than the traditional top-down one.

Finally, and this is the most delicate issue, an industrialization where the value that has to be created has to be considered not only in terms of *profits* for the enterprises that work in the market economy, but also in terms of a variety of *benefits* for the partners, who are driven by a different set of values and operate in the framework of different kinds of economies. As, for instance, the 'goal-oriented economy' of the social enterprises and the 'economy of the gift' of the voluntary organizations.

If this direction is taken a new form of industrialization will appear: an *advanced industrialization* with the capacity to coordinate a multiplicity of players to collaborate in sustainable ways, with a view to sustainable objectives, though operating on different scales and following different rationales. In synthesis, an industrialization coherent with the challenge of *the transition towards a sustainable multi-local society*.

Notes

1 *Social innovations*: changes in the way individuals or communities act to get a result (i.e. to solve a problem or to generate new opportunities). These innovations are driven by behavioural changes (more than by technology or market) and they emerge from bottom-up processes (more than from top-down ones). If the way to get a result is totally new (or if the result itself is totally new), we may refer to it as a *radical social innovation*.

2 See examples of promising cases in the Sustainable Everyday Project (SEP) repository: www.sustainable-everyday.net/EMUDE/.

3 We refer here to the results of ongoing research activities and, in particular, to the results of Emerging User Demands (EMUDE), a Specific Support Action that focuses on promising European cases of social innovation oriented towards sustainability. More precisely: EMUDE – *Emerging user demands for sustainable solutions: social innovation as a driver for technological and system innovation* 2004–2006 (NMP2-CT-2004-505345). EMUDE seeks to shed more light on cases where subjects and communities use existing resources in an original way to bring about system innovation. It aims to pinpoint the demand for products, services and solutions that such cases and communities express, and point to research lines that could lead to improved efficiency, accessibility and diffusion. Actions: (1) identify cases of social innovation geared towards sustainability; (2) evaluate, select and bring the most promising cases to light; (3) clarify the demand for products, services and solutions they give rise to; and (4) visualize, communicate and disseminate these cases and their possible implications by mean of technological trends, scenarios

and roadmaps. (End date: 31 March 2006; duration: 24 months; instrument: Specific Support Action.)

4   We have defined these people as 'creative', because they are groups of innovative citizens who are creative enough to invent new ways to solve a problem and/or to open new possibilities (Manzini and Jégou, 2003). Considering the dynamism that characterizes these creative communities we can connect the discussion on them to the old debate on the *active minorities* (Moscovici, 1979) and to more recent debates on *creative class* (Florida, 2002), *cultural creatives* (Ray and Anderson, 2000) and *creative cities* (Landry, 2000). Even if the kind of social creativity that interests us here (the creativity of citizens who are involved in creative communities) does not coincide with the one usually considered when talking about creative class or the cultural creatives, we can assume that they face similar problems and opportunities.

5   The best-known open-source collaborative experience is the Linux software, originally developed by the Finnish graduate student Linus Torvald. Anyone can use Linux for free as long as any changes or new features are shared with others at no cost. Simple rules, shared goals and clear yardsticks for judging performance, allows this global community to share ideas and, as a result, to improve the software, which is a *shared, public good.*

6   Looking at these emerging phenomena, it is reasonable to assume that the same principles of the peer-to-peer organizations can be extended to facilitate the emergence and diffusion of new creative communities and, with them, of new ideas of welfare and well-being (Cottam and Leadbeater, 2004b). On the other hand, we can also assume that the convergence between creative communities and cooperative networks can, and eventually must, be facilitated by an appropriate mix of bottom-up/top-down initiatives. That is, in order to succeed, it asks for *new forms of governance.*

7   It is important to underline that the vision of the multi-local society doesn't propose at all a nostalgic view of the past: it doesn't refer to small, local autarchic entities, but to places, communities and systems that are, as it has been noted before, highly interconnected.

8   It should be added that cosmopolitan localism generates and is generated by a new idea of well-being. This well-being is based upon the awareness of the way and the extent to which some local qualities can contribute to the possibility of feeling good; moreover, the awareness of how and the extent to which, for example, the sense of security resulting from a still-active social fabric, the healthiness of the places, the beauty of the landscape and so on can contribute to well-being (Censis, 2003). This awareness regarding the positive role of quality of context in the definition of well-being is what, first and foremost, distinguishes localism, on which we are focusing here, from the traditional local 'village culture'

(which, normally, did not attach any value to these characteristics of physical and social context). This awareness, combined with the delocalizing potential of information and communication technologies, leads to the spread of new forms of local–global activities that can readily be defined as cosmopolitan localism. Why be a broker, a musician or a potter in an undesirable place, when one can do the same in Tuscany without losing one's necessary international contacts?

9 *to distribute*: to divide something into portions and dispense it (from *Wiktionary* – the wiki-based Open Content dictionary).

10 However, for the success of this model, the place and the community, to which these products are related, need to be alive, thriving and of high quality. In other words, if there are products that carry with them the spirit of the place, the quality of this place (and of the community which characterizes it) must also be guaranteed. Therefore, a double link needs to be established between the place, the community and the product: the quality of the place and of the community is a decisive element for a product's success; and, vice versa, the success of a product, to be long term, needs to favour the qualitative regeneration of the place and the community of origin. In a few words, the products of controlled origin require places and communities of guaranteed quality.

11 The issue of local production for the local market can appear in a different context, driven by different motivation as the possibility to develop *point-of-sale production*. In this case the re-localization of a part of the production process has nothing to do with the place per se, but is a direct consequence of the search for light and flexible production systems. The possibility and the opportunity to redesign the process and the products to realize customized final products just in time and on the spot (i.e. when they are needed and where they are needed) is not new and we can refer to several families of products: from T-shirt to CD; from book to glasses; from beverages to furniture. For some of these examples point-of-sale production is now the norm. For some others the idea is still in an early phase. But, it is more than probable that the combined force of the demand for customization and contextualization, the potentialities of new technologies and the increasing environmental and economic costs of transportation will increase the possibilities for technologically localized products and productions.

12 Each enabling solution is characterized by a specific *enabling potential* that indicates how much it empowers the users and/or the communities of users. That is, how much it implements the users', and/or communities of users', capabilities to do something that they consider relevant. As, for instance:
Individuals' and/or communities' empowerment:
(1) cultural capabilities (skills and knowledge);
(2) physical capabilities (material prostheses);
(3) psychological drivers (cultural or ethical interests);
(4) economic drivers (saving money or being paid).

Improvement of context conditions:
    (1) accessibility (reducing physical or psychological barriers);
    (2) time to do it (making more efficient the proposed activity, or liberating time in other activities);
    (3) space where to do it (reducing the needed space, or liberating other spaces, or creating new spaces).
Development of systemic issues:
    (1) organizational opportunity (to support the activity organization);
    (2) network building (to support the connection between different actors);
    (3) community building (to support the building of new forms of communities);
    (4) critical mass generation (to involve the necessary number of participants).

13 Obviously, the more expert and motivated the user and the simpler the results to be achieved, the simpler the necessary instruments may be. On the other hand, the less expert the user, the more the system must be able to make up for his/her lack of skill by supplying what he/she doesn't know or can't do. In addition, the less the user is motivated, the more the system must be not only friendly but also attractive as a kind of stimulating experience.

14 The following concepts are based on the results of Highly Customized Solutions (HiCS): a European research that has been funded under the European Community 5th Framework Programme.

Bibliography

Appandurai, A. (1990) 'Disgiunzione e dufferenza nell'economia culturale globale', in Featherstone, M. (ed) *Cultura Globale*, Seam, Rome

Censis (2003) *XXXVII Rapporto sullo Situazione sociale del Paese*, Censis, Rome

Cottam, H. and Leadbeater, C. (2004a) *Health. Co-creating Services*, Design Council – RED unit, London

Cottam, H. and Leadbeater, C. (2004b) *Open Welfare: Designs on the Public Good*, Design Council, London

De Rita, G. and Bonomi, A. (1998) *Manifesto per 10 Sviluppolocale*, Bollati Boringhieri, Torino

Florida, R. (2002) *The Rise of the Creative Class. And How it is Transforming Work, Leisure, Community and Everyday Life*, Basic Books, New York

Geels, F. (2002) 'Understanding the dynamics of technological transitions: A co-evolutionary and socio-technical analysis', PhD Thesis, University Twente (Enschede), the Netherlands

Geels, F. and en Kemp, R. (2000) 'Transitions from a socio technological perspective (Transities vanuit een sociotechnisch perspectief)', Report for the Ministry of VROM, University Twente (Enschede) and MERIT, Maastricht

Landry, C. (2000) *The Creative City: A Toolkit for Urban Innovators*, Earthscan, London

Lessig, L. (2001) *The Future of Ideas. The Fate of the Commons in a Connected World*, Random House, New York

Manzini, E. and Jégou, F. (2003) *Sustainable Everyday. Scenarios of Urban Life,* Edizioni Ambiente, Milano

Manzini E. and Vezzoli C. (2002) *Product-Service Systems and Sustainability. Opportunities for Sustainable Solutions*, UNEP Publisher, Paris

Manzini, E. and Vugliano, S. (2000) *Il Locale del Globale. La Localizzazione Evoluta come Scenario Progettuale*, Pluriverso N1, Rizzoli, Milano

Manzini, E., Collina, L. and Evans, E. (eds) (2004) *Solution Oriented Partnership, How to Design Industrialized,* Cranfield University Press, Cranfield

Mont, O. (2002) 'Functional thinking. The role of functional sales and product service systems for a functional based society', research report for the Swedish EPA, IIIEE Lund University, Lund, Sweden

Moscovici, S. (1979) *Psychologie des Minorites Actives*, PUF, Paris

Ray, P. H. and Anderson, S. R. (2000) *The Cultural Creatives: How 50 Million People Are Changing the World*, Three Rivers Press, New York

Sachs, W. (1998) *Dizionario dello Sviluppo*, Gruppo Abele, Torino

Stalder, F. and Hirsh, J. (2002) 'Open source intelligence', *First Monday*, vol 7, no 6

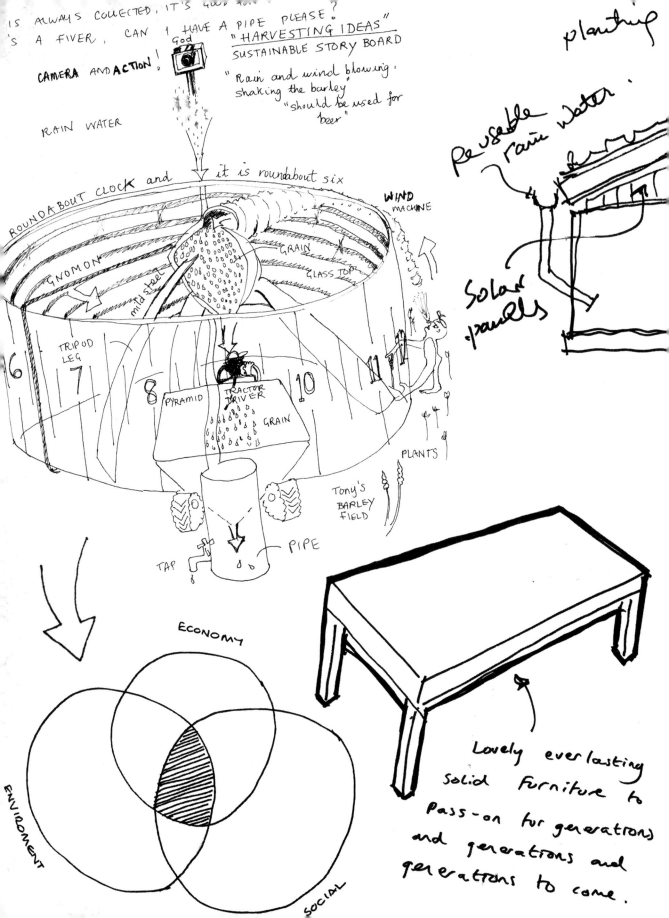

IS ALWAYS COLLECTED, IT'S GOD AND

'S A FIVER, CAN I HAVE A PIPE PLEASE?

CAMERA AND **ACTION** !

God

RAIN WATER

"HARVESTING IDEAS"
SUSTAINABLE STORY BOARD

"Rain and wind blowing,
shaking the barley"
"should be used for
beer"

planting

Reuseable rain water.

Solar panels

ROUNDABOUT CLOCK and   it is roundabout six

WIND MACHINE

GNOMON   mild steel   GRAIN

GLASS TOP

6

TRIPOD LEG   7

8   10   11   12

PYRAMID   TRACTOR DRIVER

GRAIN

PLANTS

Tony's BARLEY FIELD

TAP   PIPE

ECONOMY

ENVIRONMENT

SOCIAL

Lovely everlasting
solid furniture to
pass-on for generations
and generations and
generations to come.

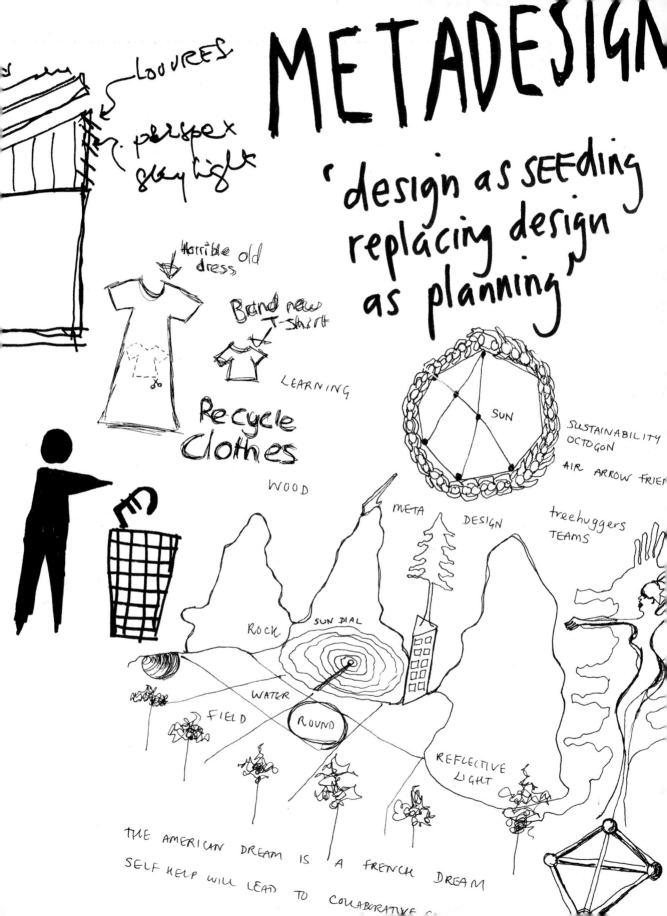

Chapter 5

John Wood

Relative Abundance:
Fuller's Discovery that the Glass Is Always Half Full

At the time of writing (2006) the UK press is scaring its poor readers with tales of human extinction caused by environmental disaster. While this is gratifying, it gives me an uneasy feeling of déjà vu. I can remember how, in 1973, the oil crisis triggered a sudden wave of public fear and alarm. For a short time I felt good. Unfortunately, within a year politicians had negotiated new oil prices and we were back in business-as-usual. Since that time the confused, myopic world of politics has hardly changed. This is deeply troubling. Despite the virtually unanimous warnings from scientists that our current living styles are causing untold harm to the ecosystem that supports our existence, politicians seem incapable of seeing positive solutions that do not involve meaningless taxes or fiscal incentives. They find it exceedingly difficult to be honest with voters where income, energy consumption, use of materials, or personal mobility is concerned. Indeed, there seems to be an unwritten law that every voter (i.e. 'consumer') has a natural born right to exploit any of these items as much as they think fit. When did this idea originate? We can probably pick any one of many key moments in the last hundred thousand years (Ponting, 1991). However, let us take a recent starting point and look at the USA's most influential export – the 'American Dream'. In his 1931 book *The Epic of America*, James Truslow Adams explored the USA's reckless craving for the good life, arguing that Americans 'were always willing to gamble their last peso on a dream'. Playful sayings like 'retail therapy', or 'shop until you drop' may not be authentically American but the political sentiment behind them is. Without doubt, the vision of new worlds without frontiers, or a money-based meritocracy based on hard work and ingenuity seems unashamedly American. Many US citizens will be displeased to hear that the American Dream is merely an echo of an older French Dream. Just before America established its constitutional terms of reference, the leaders of the French Revolution concocted a republican vision that, not surprisingly, was based on their experience of the monarchy. They decided that royal privilege had been so divisive that it should be redistributed equally to all citizens. Despite the obvious religious differences, both visions are aspirational, emancipatory and deeply humanistic. More to the point, each emphasizes rights, rather than responsibilities. How is this relevant to the issues of climate change and the extinction of species on Earth? The clue is in the three guiding principles, liberty, equality and fraternity. What is missing is any reference to 'Nature'. This is largely why we are in such a mess.

Nor can Britain's role be excluded from this analysis. It is notable that Adam Smith's influential blueprint for an economics of self-interest (*The Wealth of Nations*) was published in the same year as the American Declaration of Independence (1776). The idea that diligence by the individual will produce wealth for the many is still a cornerstone of the American economic system but, if you take Smith's logic too seriously, you may begin to value individual rights above individual responsibilities. There is a sense in which consumerism is just the latest manifestation of this creed. Today, multinational versions of the American Dream are exemplified by a dizzy plethora of readily available services, products, gifts and luxuries. This is what Bill Gates calls 'capitalism without friction' (Gates, 1999), a term that promises ease, speed and comfort, and gives a hint to what is meant by the idea of 'freedom' implicit in the American Dream. What is this 'freedom'? What would we be 'free' from? Not even the most optimistic advocate of the American Way would claim that it is a utopian Shangri-La. In essence, it is a pragmatic, money-oriented, product-centred economy. It is a place for honest hard workers who support the economy by creating jobs, buying goods and 'living it large'. In this context, freedom is the right to choose and consume, rather than to dream. Instead, professional designers dream on behalf of their customers. When this process is added to the availability of networked transactions, easy payment systems and home deliveries the consumer can choose pretty well anything he/she wants, anytime, anywhere. This reflects the tragic legacy of the French Revolution that is embedded in the dream of a Free America. Two hundred years ago, in decentralizing the monarchy as a citizen-centred republic, the leaders of the new French order wanted to give the people rights that were, loosely speaking, equal to those of a king or queen. Ideologically speaking, if cake was good enough for Marie Antoinette, or so the story suggests, it must be good enough for everyone. At that time, we needed more cake. A little later, a revolution in mass-production solved the problem. Soon, it promised to distribute luxury goods to virtually every individual.

By the end of the 19th century, designers were being asked to create new products that would appeal to different individuals (Forty, 1986). Since then, they have become increasingly important for sustaining the new American Dream. They created products that exceeded the imaginative expectations of their customers. They diversified the range of these products and made them more desirable. In so doing they diversified the market and created more business. By intervening in advertising, market research and promotional systems they created an industry that created, first, a use for desire, and then a desire *for* desire. The advent of an effective rail network, and Henry Ford's development of the first mass-produced car, created even greater potential for business and consumption on all levels. Greater personal mobility led to new vending opportunities and enterprise became rife. The American Dream became immensely appealing to the rest of the world, largely through the enviable charm, glamour and potency of the lifestyle that could be embodied and exported via novels, movies, automobiles and other products. Although some aspects of the American Way were artificially packaged for maximum effect, the system worked frighteningly well. Like many shareable dreams it became a self-fulfilling prophecy. Things could not go on like this for long. By the 1980s it was very clear that this system was eventually going to eat us out of house and home. This is why the Brundtland Report was commissioned. It was clear that the American Dream might eventually kill us all and we had to design an alternative. Thirty or forty years ago, the idea of 'eco-design' would probably have sounded a bit narrow or superficial to the pioneers of the day. By the beginning of the 21st century, potty ideas such as 'sustainable consumption' and 'sustainable business' had entered everyday parlance and were clouding the water. Today, we commonly use these terms without irony, and without apparent awareness that they might be ambiguous or oxymoronic. How, and why, did we reach this horrifying state of disorientation and self-delusion?

In the early 1970s, for those of us who were driven by anxieties about environmental catastrophe, much of the agenda was defined in terms of an 'alternative' world that seemed elusive but attainable. Today we no longer use the word 'alternative'. It was one of those idealistic words – like 'radical' or 'collective' – which were associated with a Marxist affiliation. Implicitly, 'alternative' meant 'alternative to a capitalist approach'. Unfortunately, as I have said, the idea of 'alternatives' had become unthinkable in the 1980s. Or, as Mrs Thatcher in the UK had so charmingly explained it, 'there is no alternative'. So when the idea of 'sustainability' came along, we all fell for it. Why not? For poor countries the principle behind 'sustainable development' was perfectly commendable. Once the Cold War had ended, terms such as 'alternative technology', 'alternative energy system' or, indeed, anything with the word 'alternative' in it, slowly began to lose their credibility in an increasingly pragmatic language of 'development', 'regeneration' and economic growth. Even by the time that the famous Brundtland Report arrived in 1987, the Berlin Wall was already beginning to crumble. By 1989 there seemed to be one world, rather than two, and everyone was talking about 'sustainable development'. It all seemed so reasonable. This is how things go. Given enough time it is inevitable that you will forget you are sleeping with the enemy. Before we knew where we were we had stretched the original idea of 'sustainable development' and were talking about 'sustainable products', 'sustainable approaches' and 'sustainable housing'. By now, the ice was getting thinner, and we were dressed for skating, rather than for swimming. Politically, the idea of sustainable development created the idea that there was a common agenda or consensus. If this was just an illusion, at least it might act as a conduit between East and West, between idealism and pragmatism, or between Left and Right. In reality, the single term 'sustainability' began to mutate into a set of variations, some of which were less than environmentally benign. We soon had more than 70 different definitions (Holmberg and Sandbrook, 1992; Pearce et al, 1989, cited in Boyko et al 2005a).

Where do designers fit into all this, and what have they achieved? After the Cold War, the vast majority of designers saw little option but to do what industry wanted. They created new fads, continued to design non-returnable packaging, or devised and refined new advertising techniques. Some even helped to 'de-future' products (Fry, 1999) by making them become artificially obsolescent. In short, designers became the 'fixers' who guaranteed a return on capital investment (Heskett, 1984). Those who were environmentally active were overawed by the way things were going. Most gave up the idea of working against the economic status quo and valiantly set about 'greening' the marketplace as much as possible. This shift of emphasis in the mid to late 1980s posed enormous problems for the more idealistic eco-pioneers because they soon found that even familiar ideas such as 'small is beautiful' (e.g. Schumacher, 1973) now sounded just a bit too soft, worthy or uncommercial for the new order. Many with the temerity to call themselves 'eco-designers' acquired an undeserved association with 'lentils and sandals', a taunt that was hard to shrug off in a dizzy world of thoughtless novelty and quick profits. There were mixed results. Some products, such as washing machines, became far more energy efficient, but the 'green-washing' of less deserving products and brands helped to push up sales figures across the board. The net result has been disastrous. By the end of the 20th century, the underlying tension between 'eco-design' and 'design' was becoming painful for many. By the start of the 21st century, idealism was well and truly 'dead-on-arrival', and pragmatism was the new green. This is where we are now. Today, self-deception is rife and the 'me' culture, aided by the advertising industries, has brought a consumption-oriented style of hedonism into the world. Without an alternative vision the American Dream lurches on, albeit as a pallid parody of its former red-blooded self. At the time of writing (2006), road vehicles continue to get bigger and even more preposterous, with some drivers managing to believe that their 4x4s are 'greener' than the smaller cars. Because governments have no new dream we cannot formulate a joined-up policy that is positive. Instead, threats of disaster and mindless carbon taxes are the latest TINA (i.e. 'there is no alternative').

A glance at any reasonable newspaper will confirm how deeply schizophrenic we have become. On the one hand we lament the loss of polar glaciers and ancient woodlands, or worry about the hourly extinction of irreplaceable species, for example. On the other hand we are even more terrified that share prices will drop, or that we will fail to achieve 100 per cent employment figures. Instead of discussing how we would really, really, *really* like to live, we stay too long at the office in order to do our bit for the economy. Thankfully, the mood is changing from one of confusion to fear, just as it did after the oil crisis in 1973. Let us be optimistic. Where there is anxiety there is hope, and we must make the best of this situation before politicians find a new way to distract and terrorize us with less important issues. For the moment, even in polite circles it is still acceptable to talk openly about climate change, extinction and, well, not to beat about the bush, energy wars. Perhaps the American Dream is finally in retreat. However, although the world may be about to change, designers still find themselves between a rock and a hard place. Unwittingly, they have helped to create a society of pampered individuals who believe they have an inalienable right to possess anything they purchase with their own money, and then to discard it in any way they choose.

In 1927, Coca Cola created the first non-returnable bottle, for use on ocean-going cruise ships. This was a historic moment. Like many similar and subsequent developments it was welcomed as a convenient and indispensable way to speed up economic growth. The rest of the story is far too complex, bewildering and upsetting to recount. In any case, we can all see, feel and smell the result. A more important question is how designers can best contribute to the change, in as short a time as possible. Many have been unthinkingly oblivious of the issues, or feel exempt from blame because of their specialist training. However, it seems churlish to reproach designers for their part in the disaster. The vast majority of them are let down by an education system that fails to prepare them for practice as ethical entrepreneurs, and that sees eco-design as a passing fad or, at best, a specialist subject area. Generally speaking, our failure to integrate specialist knowledge and skills has been an important barrier to the creation of an eco-society.

For me, the most optimistic scenario is the advent of a new, government-sponsored design profession that is unified within a common environmentalist agenda. For the moment, I refer to this new practice as 'metadesign'. At present most designers are specialists who have been trained to delight, persuade, pamper and mollify consumers. Few see themselves as responsible professionals on a par, say, with doctors or lawyers. This not only affects how they are perceived, and therefore how they see themselves (see Whitely, 1993), but also – more importantly – how they behave. It may make them susceptible, for example, to commercial pressures rather than to long-term social interests. In other words it makes them susceptible to parochial interests, rather than national interests, or to national, rather than global interests. It is gratifying to find that the UK Design Council's 'RED' initiative has been allowed to rock the boat a little, but where most professional bodies devise ethical codes of practice, the design industry seems more interested in asking what skills designers need to enhance Britain's economic competitiveness. It was inexcusable that the UK government's 2005 Cox Report on Creativity in Business made no mention of ethics or sustainability. And if industry treats designers like mercenaries, it is hardly surprising that most simply do what they are paid to do. This is a complex and vicious circle that is sustained by society as a whole. It is hardly surprising that designers feel confused and alienated. If the governments have failed to meet their own dismal targets on greenhouse gases, why should designers shoulder the burden by being more strategic, devious and far-sighted than the so-called experts? The education system and industry have not yet given sufficient inducement for change. Nonetheless, if, as it is claimed, 80 per cent of the environmental impact of today's products, services and infrastructures is determined at the design stage (Thackara, 2005), designers have failed to live up to their full potential in regard to the above problems. In my view, the most important question is not what kind of skills designers need, but what is their deep, long-term purpose and potential in upholding the well-being of the biosphere as a whole?

To be fair, many lone pioneers have given it their best shot. Unfortunately, even though many exemplary practices are now widely known, thanks to authors like Edwin Datschefski (2001) or Alastair Fuad-Luke (2005), this awareness has yet to transform the way that most designers practise. While some are passionately aware that we should emulate Nature (Benyus, 1997), 'de-materialize' products (e.g. Diani, 1992) or make them leaner, cleaner, slower or service-based (e.g. Manzini, 2001) rather than product-based, few of these approaches have made a lasting impression on the average designer. In the meantime, we now need a radically new way of thinking that will offer fresh visions of the future. With it we hope to transform the American Dream into a network of transient micro-utopias that will mutate and evolve like living organisms (Wood, 2007). This sounds fine, but it is certainly ambitious. It would probably call for the development of a new, consensual, holistic, non-teleological, self-reflexive discipline. This would entail an integration of existing design practices, in addition to a few more. However, what specialist designers understand as design cannot simply be scaled up without significant changes occurring. Metadesign has already been mooted as a superset of design practices and as a metaphor for emergence and control at the ecological level (Maturana, 1997). This scenario therefore places the 'metadesigner' in the role of 'systems integrator' (Galloway and Rabinowitz, 1984). According to Elisa Giaccardi, metadesign would entail a shift from normative planning ('how things ought to be') to the humanistic enterprise of seeding ('how things might be'). At a more interactive, practice-oriented level, the traditional notion of 'design as planning' can be transformed into 'design as a seeding process' (Ascott, 1994). It would therefore become more 'extensive' than design, because it would be less constrained by the specialist disciplinary constraints of product design, interior design, graphic design, and so on. It may also need to transcend the 'problem-definition' aspects of these disciplines by acknowledging and addressing issues that may fall outside, between or across the boundaries of a given issue.

For all these reasons, metadesign is not something that can simply be grafted onto our existing world without some careful reflection and adaptation. Fortunately, some of the processes and ideas needed to encourage a culture ready for metadesign are already emerging. In the workplace, for example, Gerard Fairtlough (2005) advocates the emergence of 'worker autonomy', and industrialist Ricardo Semler (2001) speaks in a similar way about what he calls 'heterarchy'. In the social sphere we have seen the emergence of the 'Walking Bus', in which children meet with their friends, get fresh air and exercise, and are safely ushered to school by foot, rather than by car. We may also have been delighted by the spontaneous and wacky antics of 'flash mobs', or pondered the wisdom of 'smart mobs' (Rheingold, 2003), 'bioteams' (Thompson, 2005), or uploaded knowledge to Jimmy Whale's 'Wikipedia'. Some of these processes evolved out of the computer industry, with movements like the 'Free Software Foundation', 'Creative Commons' and 'ShareAlike'. They all relate to what is now referred to as the 'gift economy' (Barbrook, 1998), or the 'sharing economy'. All of them celebrate the benefits of collective, unremunerated action. Up until now, our economic system has run almost entirely with a debt-based currency system. Even Michael Linton's down-to-earth 1982 currency system, known as the Local Exchange Trading Scheme, is essentially debt-based. As such these systems do little to encourage the spontaneous emergence of creative spirit, unaccountable optimism or – to use a rather unfashionable word – 'love'. In the last decade or so it is therefore encouraging to see the arrival of new processes such as 'glamourbombs' (see http://en.wikipedia.org/wiki/Glamourbomb), 'Random Acts of Kindness' (see http://en.wikipedia.org/wiki/Random_Acts_of_Kindness), or 'pay it forward' groups (Ryan Hyde, 2000). Other work is being carried out within the quest for a greater 'collective intelligence' (Surowiecki, 2004). All of the above ideas may need to be added to the repertoire of the responsible designer of the future. In some respects the growing resurgence in creativity has great potential for liberating citizens from a dreary life as passive consumers. However, this will require a shift of consciousness in which the creativity is understood as a manifold act of adaptation and integration that reconciles inner realities with their surroundings, rather than emphasizing self-expression, or delivering a flood of exotically innovative ideas or products.

One of the reasons that designers are so important is their ability to imagine new possibilities and to think 'creatively'. They can therefore play a unique and crucial role in establishing a new vision for how we can attune ourselves to Nature. In part, this is because our egotistical attitude to innovation has been responsible for much of the mess we are in. In a talk given in 2005, the architect Frank Gehry is alleged to have said, 'I don't do context'. To be fair, this was probably more of a humorous conceit than a serious statement, but it sounds dangerously like a claim to 'creative licence' in order to avoid social, political or ecological responsibility. This tendency is familiar within the history of avant-garde art movements over the last few hundred years. Many have tended to emphasize the transgressive, rather than the adaptive aspects of creativity. In many cases, it demonstrates an intrinsically amoral tendency. Ultimately, however, it has greater implications at the environmental level than at the social and political level. This is a double-edged sword. Designers are indispensable because they are 'creative'. They can create an ecological society, or they can increase profits. In some situations they can do both, but this can be a misleading expectation. Just after the start of the new millennium, creativity became fashionable in economic and political circles, partly because it was presented as the latest and coolest catalyst for economic growth. Books such as Richard Florida's *The Creative Class* (2002), or John Howkins' *The Creative Economy* (2002) reflect an enduring faith in the effectiveness of competitive, 'laissez-faire' economics. This renewed affinity between economic growth and the creative spirit is worrying, because it is part of a deeper assumption that a rising GDP will deliver well-being and happiness. This belief is what has helped to perpetuate the power of the (old) American Dream. However, the rate of economic growth has run a close parallel with the rate of discovery of new oil fields (Douthwaite, 2003). Unfortunately, it is now clear that cheap fuel is virtually a thing of the past. What we proudly refer to as 'creativity' is traditionally seen as a peculiarly western habit of thought that emerged over several thousand years. We can track it via a trajectory of ideas running from the Hellenic spirit of fierce competition, through Socratic individualism, Platonic idealism, Augustinian subjectivity, mediaeval humanism and the Enlightenment's confidence in an 'objective' and rational truth. Today, what we would recognize in the word 'creativity' is best characterized by the Romantic Movement's somewhat theatrical, confident and self-absorbed mode of thinking. In seeking a practical environmental solution for our predicament, the purpose of 'ecological creativity' is to offer the capability to adapt to our context or environment. This ability is already innate. It has evolved out of the evolutionary need to anticipate unknown conditions and to interpret aspects of a given situation in way that will prove advantageous. As such, it differs from the popular notion of creativity as merely the ability to initiate ideas, propositions or artefacts that are unique and/or innovative.

The idea of creativity as self-expression is not especially pernicious in itself, unless it is detached from a shared sense of wholeness. It is a strange idea that grew out of attempts to expand the horizon of 'objective' rationality. It represented a strongly humanistic, inward-reflective mode of thinking, that was introduced to complement the rational laws of science. We may think of this when we hear avant-garde music, or listen to 'lifestyle' interviews with a professional fashion model. Philosophically speaking, it had already taken root before the Romantic era, around the time when John Locke proclaimed, 'the mind can furnish the understanding with ideas' (1689). This tendency grew bolder over the next few hundred years, with Kant's famous challenge to the independent spirit, 'dare to know' (1784) informing the Apple Macintosh slogan 'think different'. Over this time the unprecedented idea that individuals could originate their own concepts, rather than deriving them from God or 'Nature', became bolder and increasingly strident. Since this apocalyptic era we have become increasingly adept at reinventing agriculture, science, medicine, transport, communication-at-a-distance and the experience of 'being in the world'. In the 19th century Nietzsche suggested that a sufficiently determined and creative individual might transcend the realm of ordinary mortals to become a superhuman being (German word: *Übermensch*) through his 'will to power'. We may experience an afterglow of this idea when we think of charismatic figures such as Byron, Van Gogh or Dali. We are still enthralled by the notion of a tortured, messianic genius who produces artefacts or concepts that are unique, unprecedented and awesome. This caricature of artistic superstar is a useful signifier for an extreme type of creativity that, in the past, has tended to celebrate controversy, self-importance and an emotional claim to freedom. This is exemplified by popular anecdotes about the elderly Beethoven as a cantankerous composer, tormented by the onset of madness and hearing loss. At the time that he produces his best work, he is as indifferent to the opinions of his critics as he is deaf to the actual sounds his music will make. This is a popular stereotype of creative genius that in the 20th century was epitomized by Pablo Picasso, who blurred the line between predilection, appetite and self-expression by emphasizing the importance of individual need over an external agenda, We might summarize this with the word 'arrogance'. Today, the image of self-indulgence, coupled with creativity, is now commonly used to sell products or services such as Apple Macintosh. Individual creativity has even been fetishized. In 1999, the Citroen car company bought the rights to Picasso's signature and used it to spice-up the brand value of an otherwise rather ordinary MPV bearing his name. These developments coincide, however, with changes that have also accelerated deforestation, depletion of species, pollution of air and waterways, and the exhaustion of natural resources.

They have made the threat of human annihilation a foreseeable probability, rather than a distant possibility. Today, creativity is finding its way onto the skills menu of managers, entrepreneurs and civil servants. This is not to suggest that corporate managers will become more eccentric, or that they will try to break all the rules, but who knows? Bureaucracies work by imposing meanings and habits that are constrained by epistemology, rather than by environment. This can easily lead to alienation between personal belief and professional action. If wild animals tried to live by such rules they would soon die. The introduction of a more creative culture might therefore be more helpful to the questioning of purpose, rather than for the changing of process. In reminding us that we are *here, now*, Zen Buddhism serves to reduce the disconnection between our inner values and the dynamic, living world that sustains us. It represents a kind of 'design shamanism'.

One story describes the way a good host should assess the amount of food to be cooked for her/his guests. When it works correctly, the guests are invited to eat until they have had as much as they want. When this point is reached there is not a single grain of rice left over. In effect, the experience of the guests is optimal, rather than maximal, because they can share a feeling of satisfaction in not feeling responsible for wasting food. Indeed, when a host is sufficiently shamanic to anticipate the whole event, everyone involved would probably feel more involved. This model of creativity makes an interesting contrast with our previous examples by being more altruistic and less transgressive. In Figure 5.1 we may assume that 'ecological creativity' would be in the upper right-hand quadrant of the map, and that our received prototypical 'creative' would be somewhere in the lower left corner. The need for a more complex map of relations in creative practice has emerged because our ethical systems have tended to focus on the rules of 'being' or 'doing', rather than on establishing a more comprehensive system of contextual relations. This is where the 'ecological creativity' of the Zen host is relevant. In 'guesstimating' how much rice will be eaten by others, the

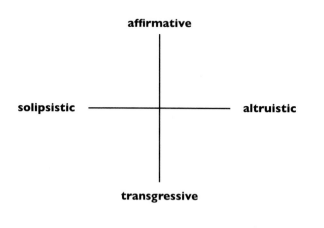

Figure 5.1 Mapping different aspects of creativity

'creative' cook works to reconcile several factors that apply in different domains. It is not a linear assessment of fixed quantities, because some factors are anticipatory. As such, they are co-contingent and require interpretive insights that are probably more interpolative than extrapolative.

One way to explain this mode of creative thinking is to refer to Charles Peirce's idea of 'abductive reasoning'. Abductive reasoning is commonly found in the average Sherlock Holmes story. Another example is the cognitive process found in 'reverse engineering'. Charles Peirce coined the term 'abduction' to account for the logic of pragmatic actions in an uncertain world. Abduction is a mode of anticipatory interpolation in which the thinker conjectures possible explanatory schema from outside the problem space in order to account for a surprising event. Mathematically, this process is akin to factoring, in which two unknown numbers have been multiplied together to produce a factor. Abductive reasoning is equivalent to deciding which numbers might have produced this outcome. This use of the notion of abduction is attributed to C. S. Peirce: 'A surprising fact, C, is observed. But if a proposition, A, were true, C would be a matter of course. Hence, there is a reason to suspect that A is true' (Wood and Taylor, 1997). Gregory Bateson (1973) suggested that 'abductive reasoning' is common within the natural order. He argues that there could be no evolutionary change and adaptation in the ecosystem without this kind of creative thinking. How can we bring the richness and colour back into this myopic method of creative thought? One way is by thinking of abduction as a 'stereo' rather than a 'mono' system – that is, by making many abductive inferences at the same time. What I call 'parallel abductive reasoning' also starts with a surprising fact (e.g. 'C') but imagines a very complex situation that might be coded as an interrelated set of conditions (i.e. A, B, C...n). Alternatively, we might imagine the answer to be a four-dimensional picture that resembles a real event rather than a 2D movie. This is where imaginative designers may be more qualified to make a new contribution than politicians and civil servants. At present, the language politicians speak is still based on the old idea of economics, and the old economic system tended to take Nature for granted.

At the national and international level, change will need to happen very quickly (Douthwaite, 2003) because the time scale of climate change and biodiversity collapse is unpredictable. If we look at the problem from a familiar economic standpoint, things seem very bleak, or even impossible. Fortunately, there are new ideas and possibilities that are lurking just around the corner. Some of them are well known or obvious. Others are subtle, and will require us to shift our expectations in order to understand and to make them work. The first one challenges the myth of economic wealth. We have known since the mid 1970s that people are no happier in rich countries than they are in poor countries (e.g. Easterlin, 1974). We also know that economic growth does not increase well-being (Oswald, 1997). These ideas have taken a long time to sink in, perhaps because money is strangely powerful, and assumes an independent existence in the form of numbers and mechanical units. For this reason it does not quite correspond to the qualities of a living organism. Hence we still adhere to Aristotle's emphasis on a 'division of labour' rather than newer visions that are less Darwinian, and which see the ecological system as a more symbiotic whole (Margulis, 1998; Lovelock, 1995; Lovelock, 2006). Similarly, the legacy of Fordism perpetuates the perceived importance of an 'economy of scale', rather than an 'ecology of scale' (Wood, 2005). In the 21st century we cannot afford to sustain this mindset. What do we mean by 'economies of scale'? This term is so widely used that it is worth exploring. It assumes that there is a reasonably linear relationship between the quantity of a given resource and the benefits that it will bring. It is complementary to the 'law of diminishing returns'. Both are essentially mechanistic models. As Alfred Marshall, the 19th century economist put it: 'the more coal you dig, the more you are forced to exploit less favourable resources'. In this model, the return for your effort is reduced because you are forced to compete with similar mines, and prices must eventually rise to meet the additional cost of production. In a sense, the old American Dream is predicated on this idea. It epitomizes a faith in 'absolute abundance'. Once you have 'exploited' a resource – say an oil well, or rain forest – you must expect an inexorable reduction in the absolute value or abundance of the resource.

The idea that the economy is more important than the ecosystem is not only bad business, it is bad for all of us. The attendant idea that Nature can be understood in terms of an 'economy of scale' or a 'Law of Diminishing Returns' are now part of a dangerously outmoded economic approach. In the 1960s, Chaos Theory led to new ways to understand the way that Nature works. It led to new theories of abundance, that include the 'Law of Increasing Returns' (Romer, 1986; Arthur, 1996). If nothing else, these theories pose a wonderful challenge for creative thinkers. They may remind us of Erwin Schrödinger's (1943) concept of 'negative entropy' (i.e. 'negentropy'), or Ilya Prigogine's theorem of minimum entropy production (1945). In these phenomena a given system dissipates some of its entropy to the surrounding region or regions. Hitherto, such ideas had tended to be regarded as being 'against the laws of nature', and on a par with fairy tales or a mad inventor's perpetual motion machine. What we now know is that Nature is far more chaotic and altruistic than we had previously thought. It is also, therefore, more fecund. Abundance is intrinsic to the world, but it may not be in familiar forms, and may not be accessible in familiar ways. Many projects fail because of tiny errors or mismatches within a large and complex whole. Often, it is clear to all the interested parties that a particular major scheme would deliver advantages to all concerned, yet there is nobody willing to initiate the chain reaction that would ensure success. Many dystopic situations are 'vicious circles' because they are configured in such a way that they reinforce and therefore sustain their own negative features. The poverty trap is a simple example. One of the new challenges for metadesigners is to know how to convert 'vicious circles' into 'virtuous circles'. This way of thinking is challenging to conventional designers, because it involves an extremely cross-disciplinary teamwork, and a highly imaginative, opportunistic approach.

Part of the system we are developing is inspired by Richard Buckminster Fuller's idea of 'Constant Relative Abundance' (Fuller, 1969). This is a controversial idea, largely because it is ambiguous. Fuller insisted that the minimum number in the world is 2, rather than 1. This is usually assumed to refer to Euler's Law, which we will come to shortly. Fuller argues that the world consists of many spinning entities and therefore, in any process of turning, there must always be two poles. Intuitively speaking, a solitary entity cannot exist unless one half can relate to the other. This is also implied in René Descartes' realization, 'I think, therefore I am', which nicely reflects the point that that there can be no point unless it is reflected. Bishop George Berkeley (1685–1753) put this in a less solipsistic way when he said, 'to be is to be perceived'. All of these insights underpin the familiar idea of a 'win–win' situation, a bi-polar situation commonly used in the world of business and politics. While 'win–win' is politically problematic because it invokes a competitive scenario implying loss, it is handy because it is auspicious (i.e. it is both familiar and appealing). Adam Smith's theory that self-help leads to collective advantage implies a 'win–win' scenario. By contrast, the fundamental sustainability argument presents a 'lose–win' offer. It is therefore a less attractive alternative. This is one reason why appeals to 'sustainability' have so far failed. But instead of applying a basic 'win–win' scenario, let us double the stakes and take four mutually advantageous aspects of a situation, rather than two. It is convenient to represent this scenario as a tetrahedron, as it clearly shows how, merely by doubling the number of components we can get six times the benefits (see Figure 5.2). 'Win–win–win–win' is a way of clustering small advantages in such a way that they synergize together and become visible enough to attract additional commitment and interest. If we view the nodes as 'players' and the edges as their 'relations', there are six times more peer relationships between four players than there are between two players (see Figure 5.2). Hence, by merely doubling the number of 'players' from two to four, we achieve a six-fold increase in the number of mutual relations that can be utilized. In short, the tetrahedron is special because it combines a graspable, non-hierarchical topology that offers possible symbiotic benefits to each of the four players.

Buckminster Fuller championed the unique properties of the tetrahedron in 1975. They were already implicit in Euler's Law (1752), which states that the number of vertices plus the number of faces in any polygon will always equal the number of edges plus two (i.e. $V + F = E + 2$) (See Stander, 1986). This '2' is what Fuller called the 'constant relative abundance'. As the surplus is always the same, irrespective of the complexity of the polygon there is a relative advantage in adopting one with a small number of sides. In the case of the tetrahedron, there is an auspicious balance between its simplicity (e.g. it is mnemonically convenient) and its relational richness (i.e. in its high ratio of edges to vertices). This can be presented to untrained users as a 'win–win–win–win' situation. This is unlikely to change until we devise a model of creativity that explicitly reconciles a number of components within a single entity. According to the British psychologist Michael Kirton, it is useful to polarize people into two extremes, 'adaptors' and 'innovators' (Kirton, 1980). According to this theory, where adaptors seek to do things 'better' using more ordered, existing terms of reference, the innovators challenge problem definition, create new definitions, and thrive on chaos. Both sets of abilities are needed within most collective endeavours. However, it can prove difficult to get these opposite characters working closely

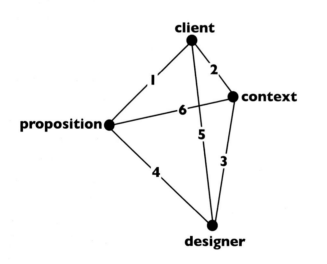

Figure 5.2 A relational map of ethical relations within design

together, because they tend to be irritated by the habits and views of the other. For example (see Figure 5.2), we may combine the following players within a single relational structure.

This is intended to enable different types of innovator to collaborate with minimum conflict:

- Designer / author / ideator / initiator
- Client / user / recipient / problem holder
- Proposition / design / idea / solution
- Context / world / background system / all that is not the task-at-hand.

Today, many are too overwhelmed by the power of the economic system to believe that tiny, local changes will have a sufficient impact. This is where we might initiate a change. In the early 20th century, any sign of positive change is a big relief to someone who has been awaiting it for 30 years. Optimism is at hand. There is even a website called 'New American Dream' (www.newdream.org/index.php) that explores the pleasures and benefits of a less wasteful way of living. But how can we sell this idea? While politicians still identify the issue in negative terms as a need for taxes and a curtailment of consumer rights, a positive remedy is needed. Fortunately, the solution may be surprising, but it is not rocket science. It is right under our noses. Some researchers have already sought to see the whole production-to-consumption cycle as a sequence of opportunities to bring the stages closer to each other, resulting in business being brought closer to Nature. (Hawken et al, 2000). The use of resources would need, ultimately, to become a 'zero-waste' system (Murray, 2002)

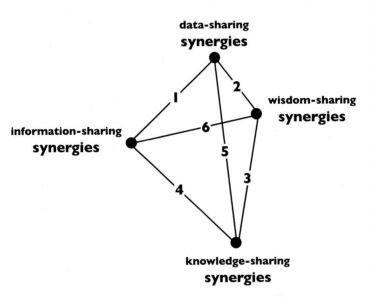

Figure 5.3 Using our 4 Orders of Synergy to map a 'Synergy-of-Synergies'

that is designed 'cradle-to-cradle' (McDonough and Braungart, 2002). The shift of view these innovations represent is beyond what we currently recognize as within the remit of any known practice of design. If we interpret this idea in terms of the existing value system we may therefore fail to understand its full potential. Within a highly corporate and consumer-oriented vision this would probably mean customers paying for their lifestyle benefits in more places, and at more frequent intervals. In short, this would mean devising a system that is decentralized, but comprehensive. This is because a less centralized alternative offers more opportunities for increasing the level of synergies within, and across the social, political, cultural and industrial domains. It would also facilitate a range of new and surprising benefits, both tangible and intangible, to be shared across a more holarchic community in which production and consumption, enterprise and altruism become increasingly interdependent. It may mean persuading producers to accept rewards that place less emphasis on income, and more on an enhanced quality of life.

Bibliography

Adams, J. T. (1931) *The Epic of America*, Greenwood Press, Boston, MA

Arthur, B. (1996) 'Increasing returns and the new world of business', *Harvard Business Review*, July/August, p100

Ascott, R. (1994) 'The architecture of cyberception', *Leonardo Electronic Almanac*, vol 2, no 8, cited in Giaccardi, E. (2005) 'Metadesign as an emergent design culture' *Leonardo Electronic Almanac*, vol 38, no 4, pp342–349

Barbrook, R. (1998) 'The hi-tech gift economy', *First Monday*, www.firstmonday.org/ issues/issue3_12/barbrook/

Bateson, G. (1973) *Steps to an Ecology of Mind*, Paladin Books, Frogmore

Benyus, J. (1997) *Innovation Inspired by Nature: Biomimicry*, William Morrow & Co, New York

Boyko, C. T., Cooper, R. and Davey, C. L. (2005a) 'Sustainability and the urban design process', *Engineering Sustainability*, vol 158, pp119–125

Boyko, C. T., Cooper, R., Davey, C. L. and Wootton, A. B. (2005) 'VivaCity2020: How sustainability and the urban design decision-making process fit together', Life in the Urban Landscape Conference, Gothenburg, Sweden, June

Brandenburger, A. and Nalebuff, B. (1996) *Co-opetition*, Doubleday Books, New York

Bruntland, G. (1987) *Our Common Future*, Report of the World Commission on Environment and Development, www.are.admin.ch/themen/ nachhaltig/00266/00540/00542/index.html?lang=en/

Csikszentmihalyi, M. (1996) *Creativity: Flow and the Psychology of Discovery and Invention*, HarperCollins Publishers, New York

Datschefski, E. (2001) *The Total Beauty of Sustainable Products*, RotoVision, Hove

Diani, M. (ed) (1992) *The Immaterial Society: Design, Culture, and Technology in the Post-modern World*, Prentice Hall, New Jersey

Douthwaite, R. (2003) (ed) *Before The Wells Run Dry: Ireland's Transition To Renewable Energy*, Lilliput Press, Dublin

Easterlin, R. (1974) 'Does economic growth improve the human lot? Some empirical evidence', in P. A. David and M. W. Reder (eds) *Nations and Households in Economic Growth: Essays in Honour of Moses Abramowitz*, Academic Press, New York and London

Fairtlough, G. (2005) *The Three Ways of Getting Things Done: Hierarchy, Heterarchy and Responsible Autonomy in Organizations*, Triarchy Press, Bridport

Florida, R. (2002) *The Rise of the Creative Class: And How it's Transforming Work, Leisure, Community and Everyday Life*, Basic Books, New York

Forty, A. (1986) *Objects of Desire: Design and Society, 1750-1980*, Thames & Hudson, London

Fry, T. (1999) *A New Design Philosophy: An Introduction to De-futuring*, University of New South Wales Press, Sydney

Fuad-Luke, A. (2002). *Eco design: The Sourcebook*, Chronicle Books, San Francisco, CA

Fuller, R. B. (1969) *Operating Manual for Spaceship Earth*, Southern Illinois University Press, Carbondale, Illinois; available online at http://bfi.org/node/422

Galloway, K. and Rabinowitz, S. (online manifesto) http://telematic.walkerart.org/ timeline/timeline_ecafe.html

Gates, B. and Collins, H. (1999) *Business @ the Speed of Thought: Succeeding in the Digital Economy*, Warner Books, New York

Hagel, J. and Armstrong, A. (1997) *Net Gain: Expanding Markets through Virtual Communities*, Harvard Business School Press, Boston

Hawken, P., Lovins, A., and Lovins, L. H. (1999), *Natural Capitalism: Creating the Next Industrial Revolution*, Rocky Mountain Institute, Snowmass, CO

Heskett, J. (1984) *Industrial Design*, Thames & Hudson, New York

Kant, I. ([1784] 1996) *Practical Philosophy*, translated and edited by M. J. Gregor, Cambridge University Press, Cambridge

Kirton, M. (1980) 'Adaptors and innovators in organizations', *Human Relations*, vol 33, no 4, 213–224

Locke, J. C. ([1689] 1998) *An Essay Concerning Human Understanding by John Locke and Roger Woolhouse*, Penguin, Harmondsworth

Lovelock, J. (1995) *Ages of Gaia*, Oxford University Press, Oxford

Lovelock, J. (2006) *The Revenge of Gaia: Why the Earth Is Fighting Back – and How We Can Still Save Humanity*, Allen Lane, Santa Barbara, California

McDonough, W. and Braungart, M. (2002) *Cradle to Cradle: Remaking the Way We Make Things*, North Point Press, New York

Manzini, E. (2001) 'From products to services. Leapfrog: Short-term strategies for sustainability', in P. Allen and D. Gee (eds) *Metaphors for Change: Partnerships, Tools and Civic Action for Sustainability*, Greenleaf Publishing, Sheffield

Margulis, L. (1998) *Symbiotic Planet: A New Look at Evolution*, Orion Publishing Group, London

Maturana, H. R. (1997) 'Metadesign', available at www.hum.auc.dk/rasand/Artikler/metadesign.htm

Moore, J. (1997) *The Death of Competition*, Harper Collins, London

Murray R. (2002) *Zero Waste*, Greenpeace Environmental Trust, London

Oswald, A. (1997) 'Happiness and economic performance', *Economic Journal*, vol 107, pp1815–1831

Ponting, C. (1991) *A Green History of the World*, Penguin Books, New York

Rheingold, H. (2003) *Smart Mobs: The Next Social Revolution*, Perseus Publishing, Cambridge, MA

Romer, P. (1986) 'Increasing returns and long run growth', *Journal of Political Economy*, vol 94, pp1002–1037

Ryan Hyde, C. (2000) *Pay It Forward*, Simon & Schuster, New York

Schumacher, E. F. (1973) *Small is Beautiful: A Study of Economics as if People Mattered*, Abacus Penguin Books, London

Semler, R. (2001) *Maverick*, Arrow Books, New York

Smith, A. ([1776] 1999) *An Inquiry into the Nature and Causes of the Wealth of Nations*, Penguin, Harmondsworth

Stander, D. (1986) http://teamat.oxfordjournals.org/cgi/content/citation/5/3/112

Surowiecki, J. (2004) *The Wisdom of Crowds: Why the Many are Smarter than the Few and How Collective Wisdom Shapes Business, Economies, Societies, and Nations*, Doubleday, New York

Thackara, J. (2005) *In the Bubble: Designing in a Complex World*, MIT Press, Cambridge, MA

Thompson, K. (2003) 'Bioteaming: A manifesto for networked business teams', Blog: www.bioteas.com

Whitely, N. (1993) *Design for Society*, Reaktion Books, London

Wood, J. (2005) '(How) can designers learn to enhance synergy within complex systems?' paper presented at the 'DESIGNsystemEVOLUTION' conference in Bremen, Germany, March

Wood, J. (2007) *Designing for Micro-utopias: Thinking Beyond the Possible*, Gower, in press

Wood, J. and Taylor, P. in collaboration with Taylor, P. (1997), 'Mapping the mapper', in D. Day and D. Kovacs (eds) *Computers, Communications, and Mental Models*, Taylor & Francis, London, pp37–44

Sustainable design can be achieved
by the 'collaborate method', because
the world is so complex and uncertain.

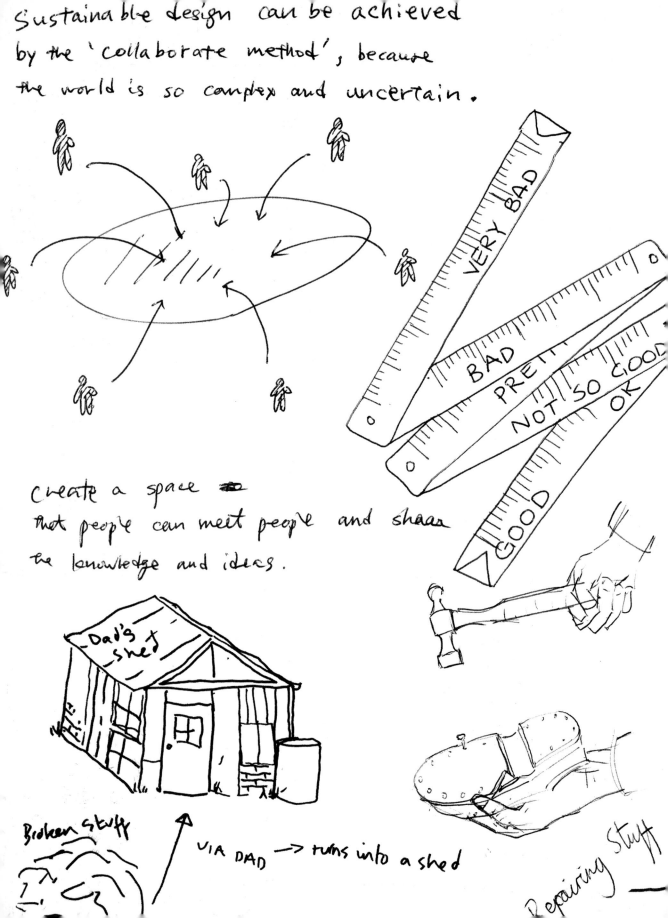

create a space
that people can meet people and share
the knowledge and ideas.

VERY BAD

BAD

PRETT

NOT SO GOOD

OK

GOOD

Dad's shed

Broken stuff

VIA DAD → turns into a shed

Repairing stuff

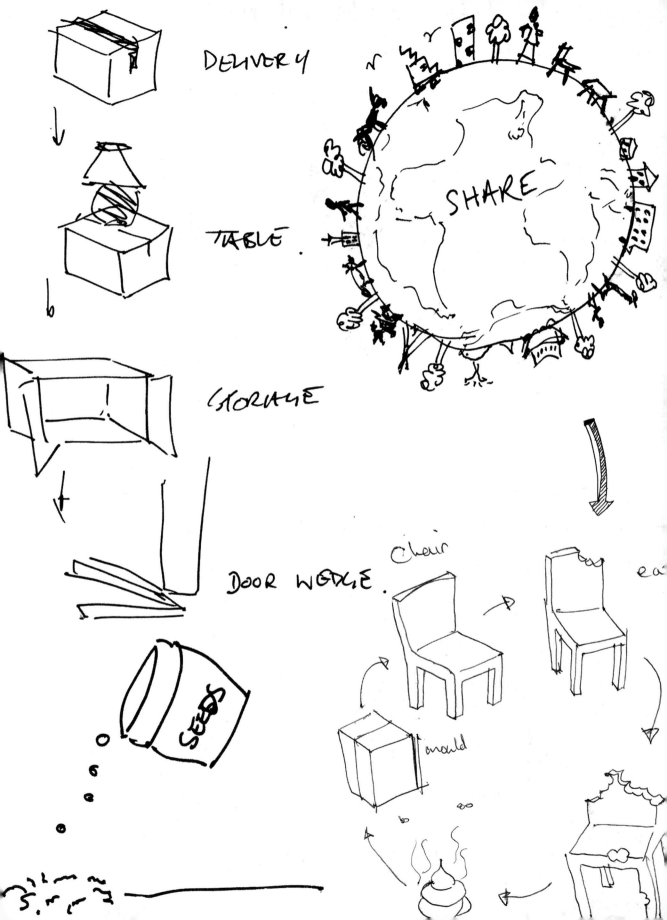

DELIVERY

TABLE

SHARE

STORAGE

DOOR WEDGE.

SEEDS

Chair

mould

Chapter 6

Kate Fletcher
Clothes That Connect

Fashion is eating itself. It has become so disconnected from reality that many of the key issues of our times – such as climate change, consumption and poverty – barely register their presence on the high street or the catwalk. Its products reinforce inequities, exploit workers, fuel resource use, increase environmental impact and generate waste. Not only that, but the sector places escalating emotional, physical and psychological pressures on everyone involved, from designers and producers to consumers. Pressures such as the drive to consume faster and cheaper, the ever-present demand for newness and the constant reformulation of identity, damage us as individuals and collectively as a society. We are alienated, dissatisfied, depressed, anorexic and more cynical than ever before.

Fashion is transforming itself. Tiny companies are making shareable clothes tuned to alternative models of social activism and aesthetic innovation;[1] giant companies are announcing plans to go carbon neutral and introducing Fairtrade cotton and recycled polyester product lines;[2] individuals are hacking the entire system, producing DIY manuals to help us 're-form' our clothes, and in so doing subvert mainstream fashion with micro-political acts of cutting, sewing and making.[3]

We live in changing times. It is up to us to steer this change towards sustainability and demand a new type of fashion based more on transformative acts and less on consumptive ones. The challenge of sustainability is slowly bringing a shift in the consciousness of consumers, designers and captains of industry. More and more people are realizing that we cannot go on as before: fashion as usual is not an option. However, this shift in consciousness is only skin-deep if it is limited to looking at symptoms of our problems rather than tackling the root causes. This paper gives form to a new vision of fashion that breaks from the past. It gets to the heart of fashion's 'problem' – our addiction to consumption – and envisages solutions that replace quantity with quality. This means shifting from global to local, from consuming to making, from illusion to imagination, from consumption of natural resources to an appreciation of the natural world. This vision is about both big and small. Each small step taken contains a tiny spark of wisdom that adds to the thinking and practice of a new way of doing things, demonstrating an alternative to the current model. The hope is that every small action in turn multiplies into support for big change.

The fashion industry

The business of producing, selling, wearing and disposal of clothes is deeply problematic. Current evidence suggests that the fashion and textile sector is among the most environmentally damaging, judged on a par with the chemical industry. It consumes vast quantities of resources (most notably water, energy and toxic chemicals); has a dubious history of worker protection; is dominated by consumption-inducing, fast changing trends and low prices that prompt consumers to buy more than they need. Recent figures suggest that in the UK over 35kg of textiles and clothing are consumed per person per year, only 13 per cent of which is re-used or recycled in any way, most of it (74 per cent) going to landfill.[4] The general trend of higher volumes and falling prices, as found at retailers such as Primark, Walmart and Tesco, means that we are consuming more fashion than ever before. In recent years the amount spent on clothing has increased while at the same time prices have dropped; thus over four years the number of garments bought per person in the UK has increased by over a third.[5]

Part of this growth in consumption is linked to an increase in speed, which in turn is only made possible by the exploitation of people and natural resources. A recent report for the international development charity War on Want revealed that some of Britain's best-known high street brands are selling clothes made by Bangladeshi workers earning as little as five pence an hour, despite pledges by these companies to protect basic human rights.[6] Speed is also linked to fashion seasons, which are now not only biannual, but each of the two main seasons contains three mini-collections, opening up new opportunities to consume. High street chains have perfected just-in-time manufacturing, with turnaround for a collection now as little as three weeks. Not only that, but the fashion trends themselves – the escalators of consumption – have repeatedly confused sustainability issues and promoted misconceptions. In the early 1990s for example, the 'eco chic' trend was dominated by natural looking colours and fibres and did not reflect real-world progress. Eco chic was more a stylized reaction against simplistic perceptions of chemicals and industrial pollution than a conversion to sustainability values. The superficial beauty, language and image of fashion trivialized the real debate and skimmed over the deeper 'ugliness' endemic in the sector, typified by a pattern of consumption that reinforces the industry's current power structures and makes fashion's ruling classes rich. Disengaged passive consumers who choose between pre-fabricated goods with no space for personalization boost 'elitist myth production upon the catwalk altar in the urban lifestyle temple'[7] and allow the fashion system to mystify, control and 'professionalize' the knowledge and confidence about the practice of designing and making clothes.

Yet we cannot give up on fashion – it is central to our culture. Fashion is important to our relationships, our aesthetic desires and identity. It has potential to empower individuals and groups, to mediate communication and to fuel creativity. Fashion can be what is set in motion when a designer presents the new collection on a catwalk in Milan. But equally, fashion can be the moment when a teenager crops a pair of jeans, adds a badge to an old sweatshirt and paints her Converse sneakers. Fashion is a magical part of our culture and a celebration of a moment where an individual is in perfect sync with time and place. We cannot give up on fashion – it is part of being human. What we need to do instead is ally it with sustainability.

This alliance involves us acknowledging the difference between fashion and clothes. Fashion and clothing are different concepts and entities. Clothing is material production; fashion is symbolic production. Although their use and looks sometimes coincide, fashion and clothes connect with us in different ways. Fashion links us to time and space and deals with our emotional needs, manifesting us as social beings, as individuals. Clothing, in contrast, is concerned chiefly with physical needs, with sheltering, shielding and adorning. Not all clothes are fashion clothes and not all fashion finds expression in garment form. Yet where the fashion sector and the clothing industry come together (in fashion clothes) our emotional needs are made manifest as garments. This overlaying of emotional needs on physical goods fuels resource consumption, generates waste and promotes short-term thinking as we turn our gaze from one silhouette, hemline and colour palette to the next. It also leaves us dissatisfied and disempowered, as physical goods, no matter how many of them we consume, can never meet our psychological needs. To change this, we need to recognize these differences and design more flexibly and intelligently. We have to celebrate fashion as the beautiful butterfly it is and at the same time divorce it from rampant material consumption. We have to produce clothes that are based on values, on skill, on carefully produced fibres; clothes that are conscientious, sustainable and beautiful.

For many people, 'sustainable' fashion clothes means functional, utilitarian garments. It means buying as few garments as possible and, when clothes are bought, sourcing them second hand, Fair Trade or organic. While this helps reduce the speed and quantity of consumption, it is ultimately a negative vision of the future; it uses yesterday's thinking to cope with the conditions of tomorrow. A new vision for sustainable fashion has to be more than a minimal consumption drive, something more attractive not because we are flippant or fashion junkies but because of the significance of fashion to human culture. A new vision will reconnect us with our clothes, their design concepts, materials and making. It will move away from the needy, destructive relationship that typifies many people's experience of fashion today, to a healthier, more therapeutic one. This view will underline the cultural importance of fashion and will champion choice, transparency and self-reliance. It will encourage a shift from the terms and metrics of quantity to those of quality – ultimately a more positive, forward-looking and creative place to be.

Inspired by Nature

This healthier, more satisfying and more honest vision of fashion's future needs design tools: tough, reliable concepts and models. Some of the most useful ones are suggested by our study of Nature. By designing around principles observable in Nature, such as efficiency, cooperation and symbiosis, the hope is that society might be sustainable in the same way that ecosystems are. Just as in natural systems, where interdependence and interconnectedness between species dominate, we would look for these same characteristics in human systems and our current culture. We can read Nature's lessons literally; and close loops, naturally recycling almost all materials, and focus on efficient use of materials. We can also interpret Nature more metaphorically and pursue designs that promote flexibility, lightness or a sense of wonder, or those that speak of balance, community values or engagement and playfulness.

Designing clothes around Nature's principles and dynamics demands diversity. There is no single one-size-fits-all solution, but multiple design opportunities working at different scales, levels, timeframes and with many different people. In Nature, diversity means strong, resilient ecosystems, able to withstand a shock or period of crisis. In fashion, it means a wealth of products and producers, different fibres and local jobs. At present, the industry is monolithic, dominated by a large number of similar garments and thematic trends. Though we may think of ourselves as spoiled for choice, most of the world's population swims in a sea of ready-made similarity. Lack of differentiation leads to boredom leads to consumption. Diversity is about not putting all our eggs in one basket. It is about designing with a range of fibres, about avoiding agricultural (and manufacturing) monocultures, spreading risk, decentralizing production, celebrating traditional fibres and giving people creative and productive employment.

Diversity demands that our fibre choices have to change. We need to substitute a variety of more sustainable materials for the socially and ecologically destructive dominant fibres of cotton and polyester (which together account for around 80 per cent of the world fibre market). This portfolio of fibre types includes natural materials like organic cotton and wool, hemp, wild silk and natural 'linen' bamboo; biodegradable synthetics like corn starch and soya bean fibre; and cellulosics manufactured from sustainably harvested eucalyptus. Evidence suggests that together these fibres offer more resource-efficient and people-friendly solutions to cotton and polyester, though they come at a cost – our clothes will get more expensive – and of course the still largely untested question is whether the mass market is prepared to pay more for such change. Designing with a greater number of small volume fibre types encourages farmers to diversify and grow a range of crops. It offers potential for regional and national fibre variation and – perhaps most critically for consumers – a choice in material type. These products could give us work and respect our local environment.

Diverse products sustain our sense of ourselves as human beings; they are heterogeneous and user-specific and recognize a wide range of symbolic and material needs. This ties in with future predictions for business more generally, which will be to find ways of satisfying the precise needs of small markets – the complete opposite of the Fordist way of doing business, where a few generic products are developed and then marketed to all people. Smaller makers with flexible production systems can produce products that are personal and specific and so they are more relevant to our needs. Homogenization and autonomy are eschewed in favour of expressiveness and difference. Diverse fashion grows out of an individual or a particular place.

The vitality of ecosystems depends on relationships and on uses and exchanges of energy and resources. In the same way, the vitality of fashion's future will be secured in the relationships it fosters. We will see beauty and greatness in garments that value process, participation and social integration, in pieces that advance relationships between people and the environment. Friends knitting together is beautiful; compostable garments are beautiful; supporting a disadvantaged community with careful purchasing is beautiful. Relationships can be fostered by designing garments that encourage us to ask deep questions about our sense of place in the natural world. Such garments could accomplish this by supporting our desire to jump on a bike instead of taking the car, or by being shareable between friends. Sustainable fashion is about a strong and nurturing relationship between consumer and producer. It is about producing garments that start a debate, invoke a deep sense of meaning or require the user to 'finish' them with skill, imagination or flair. It is about designing confidence- and capability-inducing pieces that encourage versatility, inventiveness, personalization and individual participation. It is only then that people will be transformed from blind consumers choosing between ready-made 'closed' goods into active and competent citizens making conscious choices as they buy, use and discard their clothes.

Many of these Nature-inspired opportunities lie in the re-conceiving of fashion in an industry context – not out of a philanthropic impulse, but rather because doing so makes money. There is plenty of evidence to show that embracing a social and environmental agenda increases shareholder value, creates brand equity and makes a company a preferred employer, customer and partner. In the case of giant American carpet company Interface,[8] a drive towards a goal of zero waste has saved $290 million, which more than paid for a wide range of environmental initiatives and has led to bigger profits. When companies such as Interface make legitimate returns from being 'green' they become a massive engine for change not just in the world of fashion and textiles but also in society at large. Major clothing companies like Nike[9] are also pushing corporate responsibility forward in specific ways. It has guidelines for its designers regarding materials use including a commitment to use 5 per cent organic cotton in all cotton products by 2010, a ban on PVC and a sustainable product innovation strategy. Other big names, like H&M,[10] are PVC- and fur-free and have agreed codes of conduct with suppliers to guarantee worker protection for those working in low wage economies. The largest T-shirt producer in the US, American Apparel[11] sidesteps criticism often levied at other clothing labels about their ignorance of labour and working conditions in factories in developing countries by making all their clothes in a vertically integrated mill in its own 'backyard': Downtown Los Angeles.

Even though significant momentum for sustainability is building in the fashion business, these big players can still be criticized for 'tinkering around the edges' of environmental and social problems, for making things *less unsustainable* rather than *more sustainable* by focusing on the symptoms rather than tackling a problem at its roots. Creating sustainable fashion requires profound change and radical solutions not limited to the quick fixes favoured by business cycles and profits. Of course, business can also be part of this radical agenda but a different model of business is required, not least one that asks tough questions about consumption and personal satisfaction and is based on entirely different models of individual and social action. This 'back to roots' agenda will in essence mean that sustainable fashion *will reconnect us with Nature* and *with each other*. It will reduce environmental impact, promote our sense of our place in the natural world and foster a new ethic of learning from the Earth. Sustainable fashion will encourage our sense of ourselves as human beings and reconnect us to each other, it will emancipate us and give us the skills to creatively participate with and rework our clothes. We have to become activists, skilful producers and consumers of clothes, our actions exploding some of the mystique, exclusivity and power structures of the fashion system to break the link between fashion and material consumption and to offer alternative visions of fashion's future.

5 Ways

Applying future visions to the physical reality of today's garments can take a major leap of imagination and creativity. Small signs of our readiness for this leap are all around us; in blogs, fashion magazine features, design school curricula, sustainability reporting on the stock market and Corporate Social Responsibility initiatives; there is an unprecedented interest in sustainable fashion. An important part of this leap involves creating images of and projects about possible futures or, to put it another way, offering glimpses of tomorrow to help orientate ourselves today as we make the transition towards a more sustainable future for fashion.

With that aim in mind a small collaborative research project, 5 Ways,[12] explored what sustainability qualities such as diversity, participation and efficiency might mean for fashion textiles. 5 Ways was a conceptual project producing prototypes or sketches and not fully fledged market ready products. Its aim was not to provide definitive answers to sustainability questions, but rather give some ideas and promising starting points for investigating this complex and shifting territory. 5 Ways began with a team of designers and five simple briefs. From each of the briefs and associated workshop sessions, a prototype product was developed, ranging from a leather bag to a dress. While each of these products works individually, their real value comes more from what they represent together, which is hidden from view – innovative outcomes based on sustainability values and an interconnected approach to design. The five 5 Ways projects explored:

- things made round the corner from where you live;
- things that you never want to launder;
- things that work with human needs;
- things that have multiple lives pre-ordained;
- things that require you to roll up your sleeves and get involved.

Each of these five projects is described below.

Project 1: Local

Where do you live? What are your roots? The Local project captures the essence of your area and asks you to wear it proudly on your back. It asks you to find the world in your neighbourhood and to know and support what's going on round the corner. Local products inspire and challenge the community while at the same time creating jobs and making use of local resources. The 'best' product is one with a human and material engagement with place. The 'best' product creates work at the local level that is socially enriching and economically viable. The Local project reflected a mix of concerns, some about local aesthetic preferences and others about developing products to sustain communities. These local concerns ran through all of the projects in 5 Ways: all five projects were small, informal and came from the grassroots. All adhered to the biomimicry principle of 'not fouling the nest'; using carefully selected low-impact materials and processing methods so as to keep the local (and de facto global) environment clean. The materials used in the 5 Ways project were organic cotton; Fair Trade wool; recycled polyester; and a hemp/cotton denim. These were dyed with natural indigo, heat transfer pressed or digitally printed.

Local in our case involved the design and development of products for Brick Lane, London, UK. Brick Lane has a very special character, now the centre of London's Bangladeshi community and a curry Mecca; it has a street market, acts as a base for large numbers of designer-makers and artists and is also a thriving textile and leather area. Our product local to Brick Lane evolved out of a mix of these influences. We produced a bag hand-knitted from leather scraps gathered from local workshops. The leather was cut into strips, tied together into a long ribbon and then knitted on chunky needles into a soft, tactile, extendable pouch. The bag is something to carry your fruit and vegetables home from the market stalls (shop local!); something to indicate your community identity (this is where I live!); something made from a local source of waste employing local people in the process (use waste as a resource!).

Project 2: Updatable

Fashion clothes capture a moment in time and are as quickly forgotten. But what if that moment was not one but many moments, a process of transformation? What if that process required you to reach into the sewing kit and update that garment yourself? The Updatable project is all about a switch in emphasis: from one garment to many garments; from passive consumers to active users; from a single snapshot in time to an ongoing movie. This project was concerned with the skills and confidence needed to rework a T-shirt. It was an attempt to make the process of designing and making a garment more transparent; to 'reclaim' it from specialist elite designers and to promote a greater understanding of the many small processes at work in creating a garment and encourage people to 'do-it-yourself'. Layered on top of this capability-inducing agenda was a desire to cut material consumption by recutting, restitching and restyling a piece.

Updatable involved a series of transformations to a T-shirt. Instructions, sent through the post – in our case to our team of designers – suggested modifications which keep the T-shirt at the forefront of fashion and out of the dustbin for another season. We filtered the trends and distilled them into a few smart changes. The design team then interpreted the instructions and produced a singularly stylish piece, which they documented and wore over the next months. In Updatable, the power relationship between original designer and user was changed, so that what developed was a unique collaboration based on change.

Project 3: No Wash

Behind the No Wash project was a concern with designing and wearing a garment that is never laundered. Washing clothes is, quite simply, a chore. We do it without thinking and yet it is an activity closely tied in with social acceptance, personal and romantic success and thus our happiness. Keeping clean used to be about disease prevention, but now the West's obsession with hygiene has led to the startling fact that the energy needed to wash our favourite garments through their life span is about six times that needed to make them. Just by washing clothes half as often, overall product energy consumption is cut by almost 50 per cent (and it is a similar story for air pollution and production of solid waste).

No Wash takes this idea to extremes. Here, a fine knit woollen jumper was transformed into a garment never to be washed. The No Wash top was designed partly to resist or repel dirt but mainly to wear it like a badge. It was developed in response to a six-month laundry diary, which documented majority smell under the arms and majority dirt on cuffs, elbows and front panels. The garment featured wipe-clean surfaces and extra underarm ventilation and has been worn regularly for over three years without washing. With its bold 'decoration' of coffee spills and soap smells, it reminds us of our garment's history as well as our responsibility.

Like all the 5 Ways products, the No Wash top is not a mainstream design solution, but it engages with the issues of sustainability in a new way. The complex, interrelated and constantly changing relationship between design and culture means that novel products or ways of working are not likely to come from the mainstream. Instead we need to start looking to ad hoc projects from the fringes or to alternative lifestyles. Most of us have a durable, never washed item in our wardrobes, but probably have never recognized it as such. One starting point therefore is to identify these garments' features and design to enhance these characteristics. We also need to develop alternative ways of laundering and freshening up items in parallel with designing new garments themselves. Such tricks as hanging a garment in a steamy shower room to remove odour or learning more about how stains and smells diminish, or become more tricky to remove, over time could change practices and usher in alternative models of how to live.

Project 4: Nine Lives

The Nine Lives project trades on the feline analogy and, just like a cat, which 'dies' only to live again, it sees potential in our clothes to be resurrected. We can re-use the thing wholesale; we can re-use key bits; we can rework the fibre into a new yarn; we can use it not as clothes but as stuffing for a mattress. But how can we do this so the act of giving something a new incarnation speaks to us about the cycle of life itself? Eliminating waste is a concept lifted straight from ecosystems and ecosystem-inspired design approaches like permaculture and industrial ecology, where everything is recycled and all waste from one component of the system becomes 'food' for another. Here what appears to be waste is actually exchange. The idea of exchange is a liberating one; it helps to evoke a mindset focused on getting the most out of something; and to emphasize connections, loops, cycles and forward planning.

Cycles connect things and offer opportunity for checks, balances and feedback. Cycles are everywhere in Nature, ensuring resource efficiency and balance between species. Yet to start designing in a way that 'takes a leaf out of Nature's book', a change has to be made; one that rejects the dominant (linear) industrial viewpoint that sees industry, designers and consumers as separate from the natural world; and one which no longer is exclusively focused on making a product and getting it to a customer quickly and cheaply without considering much else.

'Refurbishing' and customizing second-hand garments and fabrics into new, updated products have become some of the best-explored aspects of waste issues in fashion design. A raft of approaches such as restyling, reshaping, embellishing and over-printing give discarded, torn and stained fabrics added value, a new life and divert (or delay) waste from landfill. For example, charitable organizations such as Traid, under the label Traid Remade,[13] employ a team of innovative young designers to rework unwanted garments by transforming them into new one-off fashionable pieces that can be sold and re-used. And London-based outfit Junky Styling[14] deconstructs second-hand traditional men's suits found in jumble sales and charity shops into twisted, tailored garments. The use of vintage garments and fabrics has been a strong element of re-use partially because limited supply guarantees each piece's individuality, something which chimes nicely with the aesthetic of care and hand finishing so prevalent in re-use, but also because vintage fabrics are survivors – old things which have kept their value over time – and as such are easily associated with sustainability values.

The Nine Lives project developed garments with a pre-ordained 'future life' ready installed. The next step is envisaged, planned for and built in and the act of transformation breathes new life into a tired garment. For Nine Lives we produced two pieces that were creatively morphed into one in their next life. A knitted woollen top and simple printed A-line skirt are transformed by embroidery. Using the yarn carefully unwound from the top, and the sewing guide printed on the skirt in its first life, the user stitches into the skirt to produce a new and unique piece. The unravelling of the jumper and the making of the new skirt are deliberate acts of recreation and show us the possibilities of engaging with our garments in a new way.

Project 5: Super Satisfiers

Clothes protect our modesty and keep us warm. We also use them to signal who and what we are, to attract (or repel) others and to put us in a particular frame of mind. These insatiable emotional needs are triggers for dissatisfaction with ourselves and our clothes, and lead to an escalation in how and what we buy. Curbing the quantity of clothes bought and sold would likely have a significant and positive influence on the environmental and social impact caused by the fashion sector. But if we want to avoid depriving people of their need for identity and participation, we cannot just forget about fashion and scrap everything other than the wardrobe basics. There is no point in discouraging the buying of clothes without putting forward alternative ways of signalling who and what we are to others. In other words, we cannot radically cut consumption of clothing until we begin to understand its significance as a satisfier of human needs.

Humans possess specific, identifiable, underlying needs that are the same, regardless of nation, religion or culture. Manfred Max-Neef[15] has identified these as subsistence, protection, affection, understanding, participation, creation, recreation, identity and freedom. Crucially, while these needs stay the same, what changes with time and between individuals is how we go about meeting or satisfying these needs. Different satisfiers have different implications not only for those involved but also for external factors such as the environment. Where these satisfiers are manifest as products or services, they are the traditional (if unconscious) focus of design. The nine needs fall into two broad categories: physical (material) needs and psychological (non-material) needs. As noted earlier, we do not just use materials to satisfy our physical needs, but we also use them to satisfy our psychological and emotional needs too. This means, for example, that many of us relate our individual identity to what and how many materials we consume. Here lies a paradox: psychological needs are not easily satisfied, and in some cases are even inhibited, by consuming materials, a fact long recognized by many religious communities in their guidelines for living materially-simple but spiritually-rich lives. Yet the pressure to consume materials continues to intensify, pushed onwards by marketing, social competition and the driving forces, innate in humans, of emulation and envy.

Super Satisfiers investigated what happens when our need for identity, affection and leisure is the overt rather than covert focus of a garment. Does this begin to break the chain of consumption and dissatisfaction? Does it focus our attention on the futility of trying to meet such emotional needs through clothing or does the act of making hidden needs obvious connect us more with ourselves? The Super Satisfiers project focused on our need for affection and developed the 'caress dress' – one designer's highly personal take on how she attracts attention from others through garments. The dress uses slits and subtle cut-aways to reveal hints of bare skin at the shoulder, the waist and the small of the back. Its purpose is to invite friends to touch and for you to feel the warmth of others' affection for you.

Conclusions

What sustainable fashion needs is not mass answers but a mass of answers, and 5 Ways, while it has many limitations, is an attempt to glimpse some of this diversity. Central to the success of these ideas, and sustainable fashion more generally, is openness to the qualities and values of sustainability found in Nature, so emphasizing relationships, connectedness and cooperation. It is only then that we will properly acknowledge that ideas of sustainability require more than a focus on environmental issues to make them happen. They also require personal, social and institutional transformation and from this transformation a new way of clothing ourselves will emerge that will speak of a new rhythm and role for fashion, that will engage and empower users and not just cover their bodies, that will release industry from a potentially self-destructive, ever-faster pace of change and will herald the beginning of a way of thinking that champions the creation of a sustainable and satisfying wardrobe.

The future of sustainable fashion lies in being able to see the 'whole' and understand the mosaic of interconnected resource-flows behind a garment while still being able to act insightfully, practically and simply. We need to combine knowledge with instinct and create an industry that provides secure employment, a creative practice for designers and consumers and a staging ground for cutting-edge environmental practices. This industry will have a sense of connection or closeness at its heart; a connection to those who make or use clothes, with the ecological systems that support production and consumption and, critically, with the products themselves.

Endnotes

1   Keep and Share's alternative luxury knitwear can be found at www.keepandshare. co.uk

2   For more on Marks and Spencer's new sustainability strategy visit www. marksandspencer.com/thecompany/plana/index.shtml

3   Otto von Busch's work can be seen at www.selfpassage.org

4   Allwood, J. M., Laursen, S. E., Malvido de Rodriguez, C. and Bocken, N. M. P. (2006) *Well Dressed?*, University of Cambridge Institute of Manufacturing, Cambridge, p2

5   Allwood, J. M., Laursen, S. E., Malvido de Rodriguez, C. and Bocken, N. M. P. (2006) *Well Dressed?*, University of Cambridge Institute of Manufacturing, Cambridge, p12

6   War on Want (2006), 'Fashion victims: The true cost of cheap clothes at Primark, Asda and Tesco', www.waronwant.org/Fashion+Victims+13593.twl

7   von Busch, O. (2005), 'Re-forming appearance: Subversive strategies in the fashion system – reflections on complementary modes of production', Research Paper, www.selfpassage.org

8   www.interfaceinc.com

9   www.nike.com/nikebiz

10 www.hm.com/us/corporateresponsibility/csrreporting__csrreporting.nhtml

11 www.americanapparel.net

12 5 Ways ran between June 2002 and May 2003 and was a collaborative project

between Kate Fletcher and Becky Earley, funded by AHRB and Chelsea College of Art & Design. For more information see www.5ways.info

13 www.traid.org.uk/custom.html

14 www.junkystyling.co.uk

15 Ekins, P. and Max-Neef, M. (eds) (1992) *Real-Life Economics*, Routledge, London

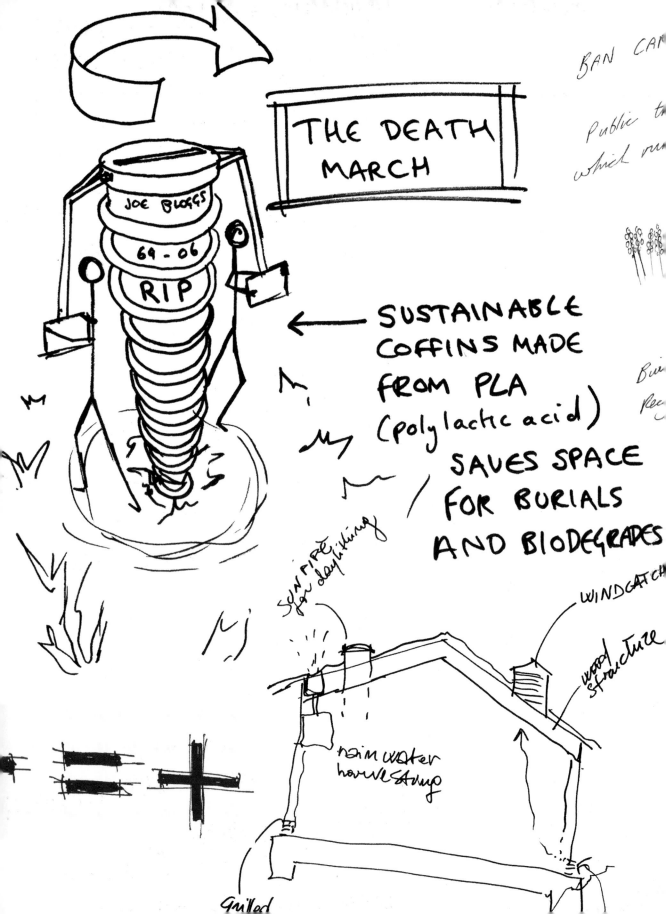

THE DEATH MARCH

JOE BLOGGS

69 - 06

RIP

← SUSTAINABLE COFFINS MADE FROM PLA (polylactic acid)

SAVES SPACE FOR BURIALS AND BIODEGRADES

BAN CA...

Public t...
which ru...

Bui...
Rec...

sun pipe for daylighting

WINDCATCH...

wood structure

rain water harvesting

grilled

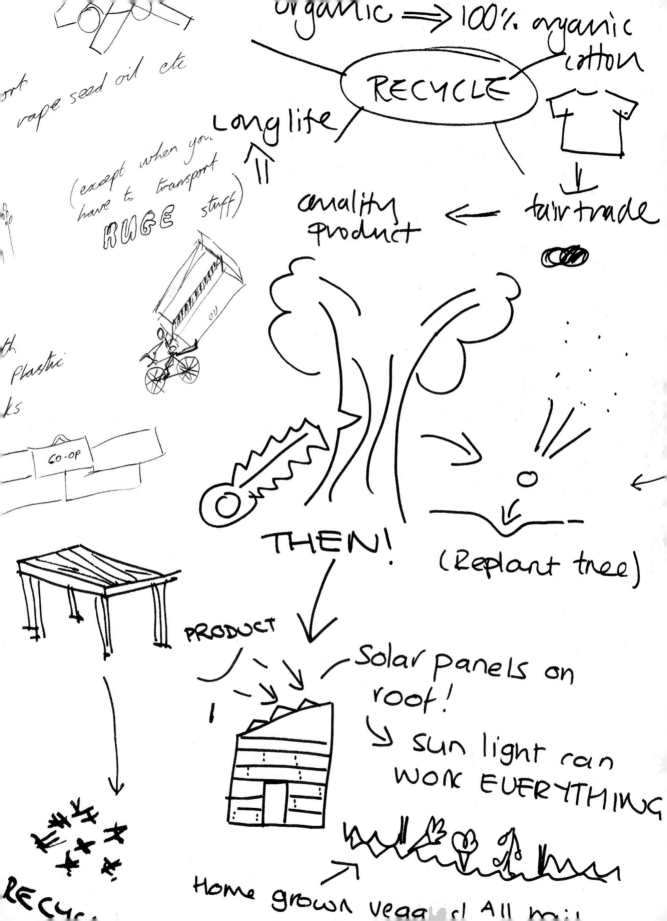

organic ⟹ 100% organic cotton

RECYCLE

rape seed oil etc

Long life

(except when you have to transport HUGE stuff)

quality product ← fairtrade

th Plastic ks

CO-OP

THEN!

(Replant tree)

PRODUCT

Solar panels on roof!

↳ sun light can work EVERYTHING

Home grown veggies! All m...

RECYC...

Chapter 7

JONATHAN CHAPMAN & NICK GANT

(In)conclusion

The creative practitioner's ability to view and understand problems and situations from a particular perspective is largely dependent on their ability to develop individual opinion and insight, relating to a given context or scenario. As a result, the way that designers *already* work is particularly well suited to the emergent context of sustainable design, as this critical process provides an essential facet of sustainable creative practice where views are an essential ingredient to progress. However, through the process of forming an individual approach and methodology, it is obvious that both *disagreement* and *agreement* will occur, forcing us to establish (and defend) our newly formed stance on a given issue. Indeed, no one knows what the world is meant to be, or look like. In this sense, how can one methodology or approach provide such a singular and absolute solution – it may even be argued that such a singular ideology should actually be avoided, as this would serve to indoctrinate and stifle an otherwise abundant and free-flowing creative culture of critique and innovation, where practitioners are free to develop, share and nurture their own approaches and visions of sustainable design.

This book aims at creating such a scenario, through the presentation of progressive, idiosyncratic and conflicting views. Through discussion, opinion is formed, sharpened and, perhaps more importantly, owned. This process of individual *authorship* and *ownership* enables the creative practitioner to move forward, to claim distinctive territories of expertise and insight – a form of engagement that enables one to establish a *practice*, characterized by a particular *individually defined* approach to pervasive issues of sustainability and design.

It has been said that a large proportion of sustainable design activity is driven by perception of what is believed to be best for the environment. This is inevitable to a degree, as in an individualistic sense perception becomes, and is, reality. Before you can change something, you must first understand it. Current understanding of sustainable design is unhelpfully fragmented and disparate, while also being based largely on what people *think* is best. These questions were posed to the members of the creative industry, which included individual contributors from the following creative sectors: product design, architecture and interiors, graphic design and illustration, exhibition and spatial design, science and engineering, education, landscape architecture, new media and digital, journalism and media, government and policy, specifier, fashion and textiles, arts and crafts, materials and design research. The results of the survey clearly showed that although levels of industry engagement and interest in the subject were high, methodologies tended to be focused on more immediate and *popular* approaches such as solar, wind and recycling. This is peculiar, when one considers the many approaches to sustainable design that are currently available today, and are still waiting to be pioneered. It was also found that although many situate sustainable design at the *creative forefront* of industry today, few actually know how to integrate and deploy it within design practice, on the ground.

Beyond scientifically grounded measures of ecological sustainability that proliferate the confines of design research and academia, sustainable design *practice* is driven largely by assumption, and preconception as to what constitutes best practice. Much of the sustainable design debate is dominated by academics and so far the content of this discussion has yet to fully penetrate the world of practising designers. For example, academic research can occupy intellectual territory that enables broad and inclusive theories to be generated, while the practising designer must ordinarily deal with more immediate issues, such as the radius of a particular curve or the way in which two mouldings interlock. Some might argue that this is simply an issue of scale, and in many ways it is.

Clearly, greater flows of palatable information are urgently required between academia and research organizations and industry. After all, where is the political social research department in the average design practice? Though such facilities are desired and dreamt of, budgets do not allow them. When considering how a practising designer can enact social change while designing a new toilet cistern, it seems apparent that further *tools* and *devices* are required to enable designers at all levels to join the debate and act upon their interpretations of progress.

The sustainable design debate has developed a preoccupation within the binary opposites of *local* and *global*. Yet, depending on one's individually experienced context, the boundaries that delineate terminologies such as *global* and *local* shift dramatically; for example, being able to establish a perception of one's position within a particular global economy, national industry sector, regional company or specific department. Boundaries are also influenced by temporal factors; for example, your individual role and effect within a financial year, a good month, a busy week, a hectic hour or this very second. Of course, within any of these scales, engagement is important (regardless of their 'local or global' character), but it is essential to be able to establish a clear perception of one's individual 'place' within any given time or space as, through this, appropriate ways of working can be identified and deployed. Terms such as *global* and *local* are useful, yet their implied scale is 'context dependent'. This ambiguity can be both positive and negative in terms of defining your working environment. In one sense, it jams progress through the promotion of gross generalizations that inhibit action because of their over-facing and insurmountable nature. However, in another sense, understanding your relative place within the *bigger picture* can be helpful if it enables the definition of one's capabilities and potential to influence positive change. In this way, absolute terms such as *global* and *local*, *sustainable* and *unsustainable* must be handled with care and consideration.

Sustainable design is a debate the fundamental principles, philosophies and working methodologies of which transcend disciplinary boundaries. Yet, cooperative design methodologies remain *slaves to scale*, in that as production volumes escalate to satisfy a proliferation in consumer demand, inclusive strategies for co-design become increasingly difficult to nurture; however, the underlying principles of collaborative networks are already an established and fundamental facet of current economic models that need retuning at the specification stage. There are scenarios where it is appropriate to include the end user in the process of creation or to engineer social situations. For example, if you are a team of architects planning a suburban school, it may be appropriate (if not essential) to engage the residents of that locality in the creative process. However, if you are currently part of a product design team developing a new ring pull for the world's soft drinks market, the potential for such bespoke processes drops promptly – nonetheless, you are still part of a network that can be positively and appropriately modified in response to a given project and ecological ambition, regardless of scale.

In recent years, there has been a steadily increasing shift in focus, towards the emerging manufacturing superpowers of the developing world. The growth of these *new polluters* seems commensurate with a reduction in control, as manufacturing bases become increasingly remote; this is forcing many to question, 'what is the point in improving if these improvements are overridden in this way'? Yet, as some developing economies continue to replicate western models of production and consumption, leading by example, rather than waiting for *each other* to change first, becomes a more effective and forward-facing practice. If we (in the developed world) are the leading economies demanding sustainable goods, then surely, providers of these goods will be motivated (through economic incentives) to produce *more* sustainable products, as that is what is being demanded. This is a simple principle of *supply and demand*, and also relates well to the philosophical notion of *being the change you wish to see in the world*. Furthermore, if the economic driver that is so often the catalyst for *unsustainable activity* within industry were to be reversed, it would automatically become the very driver for *sustainable activity*. Such cultural change (represented by this proposition) acts as a snowball, harnessing a momentum that is difficult to stop; at which point, the only option is to *steer* and *direct*.

The impact of sustainable design so far has been limited, and the real potential it holds has yet to be fully activated. Designers have a new purpose, and new and visionary cause to champion. In this way, sustainability should not be seen as a problem, crisis or challenge; rather, sustainability is an unprecedented opportunity for Design to reinvent itself, giving new purpose, direction and motivation. In today's competitive market, an increasing number of multinational companies see an economically viable and competitive future in eco-efficient products and processes. This is due to growing market demand, fuelled by the growing tangibility of our ecological impact, combined with rising cost of energy and resources and the leverage of current and forthcoming environmental legislation. In this sense, we (as an industry) must no longer be cautious in our engagement with sustainable design. Now is the time and the place to embed these considerations within the proposal of new products, spaces and experiences, and their positive relationships to both economic and sustainable growth; ample evidence exists that indicates their compatibility with commercial processes and a more stable economy, long term.

As with any commercial organization, goal-oriented organisms, or ecosystems, are dependent upon diversity and pluralism to survive and prosper. A variety and multiplicity of elements provide the core of such cultures, and in this sense the very notion of stability is both obscure and alien, as it serves primarily to homogenize, and therefore exclude. Rather, progressive systems must be constructed upon a rich and diverse foundation, in order for *cultural well-being* to manifest within sustainable design; sustainability becomes a culture in and of itself, with values, beliefs, legends, folklore and *other stories*. One thing is certain – without debate, agreement and disagreement, this enriched and thriving *multiculturalism* in sustainable design will remain a tantalizing yet unachievable utopia.

On an individual level, the designer is both a consumer and producer of things, and these dualistic roles are co-existent, and ever present. This is because in order to produce finished, resolved objects one must consume (often through specifying) materials, components and manufacturing processes. In this way, it can be seen that much of creative practice is the practice of appropriate consumption – the acquisition, combining and processing of *existing things* to enable the development and production of *new things*. As such, the designer has the same choices (if not more) as the average high-street consumer, though the responsibility is far greater due to the multiples being dealt with in production scenarios. An unsustainable choice made by a shopper on the high street is multiplied by only the one product purchased, whereas an unsustainable choice in the design studio might be multiplied by as many as 10,000 depending on the production volumes in question. So, designers must lead by example, shopping local, choosing recycled and considering the appropriateness of all things, if the right changes are to be made – after all, *sustainable consumption* is only really achievable when there are sustainable products and services for us to *consume*. Whether a sustainable designer or not, it is clear that all designers are in a crucial position, with unprecedented influence over the sustainability (or unsustainability) of design, production and consumption today.

The design process provides points of intervention for sustainable progress that serve to punctuate the broader process of creative practice as a whole. It is often the designer whose central role establishes the underlying conceptual orientation, and driver, for a given product, which in many ways is where the most significant developments lurk. Designers also have a degree of governance over the life span (and life cycles) of the product in terms of both its *physical* and *emotional durability*. This might include biodegradability and the potential for re-use and recycling of materials and component parts (physical durability) or less tangible means such as designing objects that *grow old gracefully* and that are capable of sustaining a more durable relationship with the user (emotional durability). These considerations have great impact on the environment through both the avoidance and reduction of waste.

Supply chain management methodologies are also at the designer's fingertips; a UK-based designer specifying recycled acrylic from South Africa might suggest room for improvement, and buying (or specification) choices such as these underlie practically all consumer products available today. The importance of manufacturing processes as a point in the design process that has impact cannot be over-emphasized; crucial considerations underlie the specification and use of a particular approach to object creation, both in terms of the utility of the object and its ecological impact. In this way, possibilities for sustainability are largely dependent on how objects are manufactured, and this can be achieved only through individual practitioners applying an engaged, tacit understanding of how things can be made, from what, and at what cost in the context of energy consumption, subsequent resource depletion and atmospheric pollution.

Form and function of objects play a central role in the practice of any designer. The function of an object is central to its success and presents creative practitioners with a multitude of opportunities to embed sustainability within their output. Form plays an integral role in achieving functionality – the two are interrelated. For example, a stackable chair that is made from sustainably sourced timber becomes a strong and durable yet lightweight piece of furniture that is efficient in terms of transportation and the consumption of materials and energy during manufacture. This demonstrates where *form* has a vital role to play in achieving the *function* of sustainability.

Function also has a more ethereal quality and it could be said that function exists on a linear scale, in which at one end you have *task-oriented function* where objects perform and fulfil their tasks well (which is a sustainable characteristic), and at the other end of the scale you have a more *sociological function* where objects are effective in mediating the particular values and beliefs of the user. Both modes of functionality are largely dependent on the designer, and are central to the success or failure of an object in social, economic and environmental terms, as when objects succeed within both modes of functionality through design, replacement motives are quelled, and things generally, are valued, cherished and kept. Marketing is part of the design process, where the sustainable attributes of product outputs are to be identified and celebrated, leading by example to make sustainability the new consumer language of *desire* and *obsession*. Packaging and distribution (or ideally, the lack of it) are also largely at the designer's disposal, and could relate positively to all of the above fragments and elements of sustainable design practice, if done correctly.

When one looks holistically beyond these incremental parts of the design process, one can see that designers also have the ability to engage with more overarching, systemic approaches that develop new consumer paradigms (and even entire socio-cultural *movements* and *behaviours*) to provide a further layer of intervention for creative practitioners to engage with. When one considers this diversity of roles, the importance of the designer within the creative sustainable system becomes apparent. Furthermore, when one considers the pluralistic context of design practice, it appears somewhat 'obvious' that sustainability was made for the design industry. Designers already work in this way – adapting and progressing current ways to achieve desired futures – so in this sense sustainable design sits particularly well within the context of everyday design activity. It can therefore be asserted that designers are key-holders, situated within the nucleus of the sustainability debate, and not purveyors (or procurers) of bolt-on after measures that simply apply damage control, but never really gain any ground on the issue.

Most manufactured products fail to personify and articulate the process embedded within them and, consequently, fail to include the user in the story of their creation, or genesis. As a result, new opportunities emerge for the development of new objects that mediate the story of sustainability in a more tangible and inclusive way, feeding and fuelling the *awakening consciousness* of a consumer populace in search of products boasting greater ecological integrity. This is not to say that *black-box* anonymous products must be outlawed and driven out of town, but rather, there is room in the market for alternatives that offer a more inclusive vernacular. The question must be asked, 'does (and should) sustainable design have a language, and could such a prescribed aesthetic be obstructive in streamlining consumers into two opposing profiles: those that buy green, and those that do not?'

Consumers are becoming increasingly astute in their ability to distinguish authenticity, so the danger of misinterpretation of inauthentic claims of sustainable credentials could be described as unlikely. However, it is essential that sustainable design does not become an inauthentic stylistic era of design; as with any era (or trend) it will ultimately fade away, through familiarity, overuse and a failure to impact. In contrast, if a tangible sustainable design attribute of a product is well articulated and clearly presented through the object, an aura of authenticity is generated that sets a precedent, while transcending ingenuous duplication. When objects embody characteristics such as these, an eco-nomic marketable value is also accrued that links fluidly with commercial success. Market demand has driven prices down and productivity ever upward, and now this established model of progress is being drawn into question. This situation poses a wealth of opportunities, as established methodologies immediately come up for questioning, review and potentially, change.

For a while we were seduced simply by the beautifully hyper-real objects modelled within virtual environments, and for some time this futuristic preoccupation with polymer-skinned artefacts was satisfactory. Increasingly though, consumers hanker for more meaningful content within the material fabric of their lives. This is due to the fact that the narrative experience of objects has become stripped out of consumer products to enable them to anonymously demand no emotive connection other than that which the brand enables. In these scenarios, two key things have been inadvertently *plucked* from the vocabulary of objects – *craft* and *quality*. Craft as a practice has been all but replaced by the streamlined processes of mass-production; this has enabled the creation of a homogeneous and glossy domain where anonymous objects flood the made-world with a monosyllabic drone – which contradicts the very notion of design as a celebration of independence and creative self-expression. Not to say that we should all lovingly buy rickety wicker baskets, and hand-turned oak eggcups – particularly if you are a vegan with no need for an eggcup – but considering how, and from where, things are made is virtually impossible for consumers, without such ready information imbued within the objects' gestalt aesthetic. New paradigms must be created, fuelled by the underlying ecological predicament, orchestrated by the designer who sits at the heart of a network of all stakeholders.

As the term *debate* implies, the *sustainable design debate* is inconclusive, by its very nature. This inconclusive character is essential, as without it, the debate, discussion and critical nature of sustainable design instantly shuts down, putting an end to growth, development and evolution of thought; as such, (in)conclusion is, and should be, the state of play, as without discussion, evolution and progress stagnate. This is not to say that decisions and assertions should be avoided; rather, decision should be approached as an integral (and essential) part of design. *Effective* design does not stop criticizing and improving – it is an iterative, ongoing process of serial-evolutions, rather than a one-stop, big bang fix-all scenario. Therefore, it would be wrong to conclude – conclusions make answers, conclusions are subjective, and this is often non-inclusive. So, what would your contribution to this book look like? What would you argue, defend and propose, and why? How would this change the debate? One thing is sure; an inclusive culture of critical debate and engagement is necessary if real positive change is to be fostered by today's designers and visionaries.

A

B

C

D

S